STREET SMART KIDS

Common Sense for the Real World

for ***ordinary*** kids who would like

to be**...*EXTRAORDINARY!***

Dedication

A special thanks to my wonderful friends and family who have encouraged me, given me their insight, and supported me even though they originally thought that I could not and would not change the world! And especially to Ami, Cheryl, Bill, Roger, Gina, Victor, Ron, Donna, Brad and Jack who read the manuscript before it went to press and gave me their honest opinions, which I, of course, took very seriously. ;)

This book is also dedicated to my remarkable wife Alice, our two children Talia, nineteen, and Dustin, sixteen who all constantly fill me with exhilarating pride and joy. My most cherished moments are being surrounded by all who give my family love.

And an extra special thanks to those initial strangers who have given me the time of day, accurate directions or good advice, returned my calls, been punctual, looked me in the eye, and listened when I spoke.

Without you there would be less hope and less proof that people are generally good and are still looking for a place to share some love without getting kicked in the teeth for it.

Contents

"The way we *see the problem* is the problem."

Dr. Stephen R. Covey (1932-2012)

Foreword

As a kid growing up in Namibia (southwestern Africa) until the age of seven and then in Cape Town, South Africa, until twenty-five, I was always curiously inspired by the many stories I heard from people who were fortunate enough to enjoy the good things that life had to offer, especially those who went anywhere overseas, a journey of at least ten thousand miles. It was a huge undertaking if you lived at the southernmost tip of Africa, unless you had the means to take a very, very expensive trip.

Being from an economically challenged family and never having ventured beyond the "bottom of the world," I relied solely on what I saw in the movies and read in comics that depicted life in the rest of the world. Being an adolescent, tucked away in Southern Africa, my life was the epitome of "behind the times." With limited practical exposure to a global culture and living in TV-less isolation, I was growing up in the dark with no idea that there *was* a light switch.

Filled with irrepressible energy and a very strong will, it was tough to keep a lid on me. I needed far more attention and stimulation than was readily available to a kid in my position and so, consequently, I did not grow up well-adjusted. I was engulfed in a tumultuous environment laden with rebellion and destruction, leading to an unavoidable early self-dependence.

Additionally, as yet another product of a seriously broken home and having to endure the effects of a far from warm and fuzzy family life, it was no surprise that by the time I had finished high school, I had found myself in and out of all kinds of trouble. The absurdity is that I had attempted almost everything that a naughty, frustrated kid could possibly dream up, at least once or twice, but without getting caught *too often* and, therefore, mercifully avoiding what any sane person would consider to be really serious consequences.

No doubt, some of the most harrowing experiences that I was fortunate enough to escape from (and now, somewhat sheepishly, look back on), warrant the utmost attention; I feel compelled to share them and spare anyone who might be heading down a similarly contaminated path.

This pattern of testing the system continued beyond my school years and especially through two years of mandatory military service where it became exceedingly obvious that I was one very reckless yet fortunate human being. Your hair might stand on end if you or your kids knew someone like me or if they joined me in some of the irresponsible antics that were a part of my daily routine. I pushed the envelope to places it had rarely been. Looking back today, boy oh boy, what outlandish but exhilarating entertainment!

With dreams and aspirations to have what others had, I finally drummed up the courage and resources and left South Africa to explore the rest of the world, alone at age twenty-five. With nothing but a very full backpack, some cash, and hoards of Transkei-made jewelry to sell (to beat the horrific exchange rate), I was heading anywhere with no plans to return anytime soon. I spent eight months winging it through eleven different countries, living an unpredictable and inconceivable experience of a lifetime...and then some!

As you might imagine, arriving in the United States, completely alone and with about $225 to my name, I was quite unprepared for life in Los Angeles, California (or anywhere really for that matter). I had to take a deep breath or two and figure out what to do about this overwhelmingly complex dilemma in which I now found myself. Stranded, encumbered or not, I was neither in any financial position nor in any frame of mind to leave this fairytale that I was in and, besides, where was I to go anyway? Emotionally soaring and egotistically challenged to "make it" in the States, I had to walk the walk or I'd have to run back to South Africa with my tail between my legs, a place that I vowed never to raise my kids while still serving in the military. I had told my family and my friends that I was off to make my fortune in America, and I was not about to go back a failure, no matter what.

I did any and everything legal and honorable to make a buck—even if just to stay a while—one day and one dollar at a time. Twenty-six years later and still here, it is fair to say that what I learned "on the streets" is well worth sharing with others.

Now, as a grown family man, I can honestly say that I still very much want my own life, but I have come to know far too many others along the way—educated, wealthy, and privileged or not—who *would rather have my life than their own*. What an eye opener— and a strong indication that something is very wrong with our society, wrong enough that it is worth doing something about it!

How come everybody is not living at least some of the good life in the United States?

I will therefore share some of the revelations learned on my own path to appreciation and help a few kids as they shape their own life journeys, kids who perhaps also started out with inadequate tools or less parental guidance than is typically desired.

Street smarts are no doubt a strong factor in the prevention of some of the hard knocks that you are destined to experience. Life is hard, but we absolutely have to survive. Since we all want to laugh and rejoice sometimes, it is imperative to know more about living life in the "real world". After all, we are eventually going to be left to our own devices.

If you are interested and open minded enough, first understand that by just simply thinking first, many of you will avoid or better manage the pitfalls that can potentially end in serious or irreparable anguish. Sure, our own experiences teach us valuable lessons, lessons that cannot be learned in any other way, but in today's fast-changing world, there is limited time or sufficient resources to fix some of our worst mistakes. In fact, some of our choices will simply turn our lives upside down, perhaps never allowing us to fully recover.

Broken homes, broken dreams, and broken promises are all too common for too many young adults. This, in turn, leads to adults with problems—serious and unnecessary problems that contribute to the demise of today's modern families and communities.

Therefore, allow me to share some invaluable insights and spare you some of the misery of learning too much the hard way. Life should be good, very good, if not amazing—really! It's just a matter of planning it that way.

A good opportunity exists in every bad situation, no matter how bad, and I can show you how to find it, every time!

Seriously consider taking the time today to learn how to make choices that lead you to really wanting and appreciating the very life you have, *always*.

Street Smart Tips

- Almost everything learned at a young age will be much easier to retain than what you learn when you must, especially when having to break bad habits!
- Many costly mistakes are avoidable with just seconds of prior contemplation and by asking one important question. (The question and answers are to be found somewhere in this book! ☺ or visit www.streetsmartkids.com).

Preface

This book is based on one very *simple* premise: we are all surrounded by older people everywhere, and each one is a potential teacher. Their collective experiences in all facets of life far surpass anything that an individual is capable of learning alone. It is also fair to say that one can learn something from every living creature.

Sometimes it is an obvious lesson, <u>but more often it is not!</u> The most critical learning is typically gained from the good or the not so good that you are willing to recognize and appreciate when associating with others.

As one navigates through life, it really does not have to be so difficult or exhausting. *Street Smart Kids* presents a chance to experience a more fulfilling, less stressful existence for·everyone, starting right now.

With nothing to lose—and at a minimum, something worthwhile to adopt—please enjoy these thought-provoking chapters and take a few of the messages that you do like and apply them, live them and share them with someone you care about.

So you have a few problems. Guess what? So do I, as do others...accept it!

Problems are a fact of life. Almost every invention, activity, and daily task came about as a result of one problem or another, which means there are basically two kinds of problems to consider: problems that can be solved with resources (if you have them) and problems that can't.

.

*The ones that can't be solved with resources are best solved by prevention, made possible by the implementation of some measure of **street smarts** or forward thinking. Let me explain as you continue to read these short but invaluable stories and ideas.*

It is hard to believe that anyone who reads this information will not walk away a little wiser, armed with a few common sense ideas that will likely result in a few smarter choices along the way.

Nevertheless, the following anecdotes are based on true stories derived from personal experiences as well as the many, many lessons from those I have been fortunate enough to meet along the way.

My aim is to share these valuable "lessons learned" from those who have been there before you.

Given what today's generation of preteens, teenagers, young adults, parents, leaders, coaches, mentors, and teachers have to deal with, just one good idea put into practice can change the course of a life or two—maybe even yours!

Street Smart Tips

- *If you think that you are old enough to smoke, drink, drive, have sex or watch X-rated movies, then you absolutely must be old enough to take what is in this book very seriously.*
- *Don't underestimate the value of anyone's experience.*
- *Conventional education is not enough in today's world.*

Acknowledgments

To those people in our world with good intentions and living enviable lives...thank you for the inspiration!

And to those people in our world with less than admirable intentions and far from enviable lives...thank you, too, for the inspiration!

Important Notes!

1. It is highly recommended that everyone graduates from <u>a college or an accredited educational institute of sorts</u>; *however*, most of what you find in this book *cannot and will not* currently be learned at any school. A college degree may not be enough anymore!

2. While it may not be realistic to expect to live a perfect life one day, every day we *are* given opportunities to make our lives (and the lives of those around us) better, opportunities that come in all shapes and sizes from the least likely places. These opportunities are easy to grasp and, typically, only restricted by one's desire and attitude toward some of life's choices. When confronted by the many familiar circumstances that make up "life," a small shift in one's approach could positively change the outcome of many a struggle or any important decision about anything—really!

3. This is your chance to reevaluate the daily routines that are so often misinterpreted, ignored, or taken for granted. Failing to recognize their overall significance can result in some heavy consequences. The following pages are loaded with food for thought on how to get along with good people from all walks of life and how to be that person others want to be around, rather than the one from which they want to run a mile.

Chapter One

What are Street Smarts?

The expression "street smarts" is often misunderstood or misinterpreted. Of course, we are all taught to look left and right and then left again when crossing the street, to be careful around water or fire, or not to help creepy-looking men find their lost puppies. The reasons we are taught these lessons are obvious to most, especially since they have previously yielded clearly identifiable and immediate catastrophic results.

People with street smarts have developed a keen sense of *situational awareness* that has afforded them a distinct advantage over others as they steer through life's network of opportunities and obstructions. The profound rewards of having street smarts are always evident and, thankfully, never disastrous, but the ultimate expense of *not* having street smarts is not so obvious until it's pretty much too late.

Don't you find that some of life's most valuable lessons have been learned by banging your head or repeating mistakes from which you are supposed to learn? Why is it that some people struggle to become successful in life and, despite their willingness to work hard and do a satisfactory job, they seldom move beyond living from paycheck to paycheck? Of course, that is only if they are lucky enough to actually be employed.

A number of factors determine your level of awareness or your degree of street smarts; each one is a little different but as important as the next.

Some examples are: how well you know both sides of a story before providing your opinion or investing your time; how well you really know someone before considering them a true friend and trusting them; and how well you research an opportunity before investing time, money and sweat equity. It all boils down to how much you are prepared to learn, whatever you come up against.

Countless opportunities are lost every minute of every day due to a lack of preparation and a clear perception of what our fast-paced world is demanding from us. You need to be aware.

First clearly understanding the significance of a given situation and then acting appropriately is the essence of creating your own luck. Have you ever wondered how so many men and women without a formal education, with minimal resources, or with language disadvantages can become immeasurably wealthy or well grounded, while an Ivy League school graduate may struggle to find a meaningful career? The answers to these questions lie in a sphere of objectivity, common sense and simple logic.

As an example, today we are facing deeper dilemmas in our educational system that can no longer be ignored. College tuition is at an all-time high, as is the number of graduates who are either unemployed or underemployed. If you've borrowed money to attend college, you might be faced with between fifty and one hundred thousand dollars in loans. Low interest rates or not, without a job, you can't even begin to make a dent in the loan.

As your financial situation becomes worse, pressure mounts, and trying to find a good job now becomes your full-time job. Even if it takes a year to find a decent job, your debt has increased, and there is now another class of graduates on the lookout for employment. Considering the competition, if you are lucky enough to be granted an interview, you had better be very prepared!

Or, let's assume you finally do accept a position, any job you can, despite your degree in communications or your MBA. You now earn a third of what you expected your college degree to provide. Consequently, you no longer have the time to go job hunting and you still can't pay back your loan because you barely have money for food, rent, and transportation, and so you get discouraged and, quite frankly, fed up with trying. You are stuck! Moreover, the one or two dream jobs that were out there for you are snatched up by someone else because perhaps this person was fortunate to have different circumstances or was in the right place at the right time; perhaps this person had connections, did not give up or just interviewed better than you would have anyway.

This example is a slice right out of real life. There will be more opportunities for some than for others, which is why you must develop a sense of street smarts. Traditionally, it was the wise old man that one once consulted for advice, or your parents, grandparents, or relatives. But today, they no longer have all the answers because the world has actually passed them by in some very critical areas. Although they can always provide some support, they can no longer be solely relied upon to show you how it all works.

Additionally, what was once a world that lacked or suppressed invaluable information is now a world of overwhelming and sometimes paralyzing abundance. The so-called guarantees in life are gone and what was once considered the best approach is now just one of many possibilities.

But how does one sort it all out? What is real, and who is truthful? Is the information we are bombarded with reliable, or is it just another one of the numerous scams out there?

It is more important than ever to be aware, to understand the way things work, and to adapt to the rapidly changing dynamics of the new world. Some of you will make things happen, some of you will watch things happen, and then some of you will simply wonder what happened. Which one are you?

Why Do You Need Street Smarts?

Since the bar has been raised; it is no longer possible to assume that everyone has good intentions, a good attitude, and a good work ethic. You can no longer take for granted that all people can be trusted to keep their word, take responsibility, and make good on their promises to help you or make your life easier.

Faster than ever before, people are being dismissed as not worth the time and effort. If you are not bringing something of real value to the table, your seat will already have been taken. Those with substance, integrity, and dependability will be the only ones taken seriously. Accountability is no longer optional; it is required.

So how do you gain experience without actually having the experience and learn what it takes to rise to the top? Why are some being left out in the rain, while others seem to be raking it in? The rich get richer and the poor get poorer and "there ain't no middle class no more" is more relevant than ever. What exactly does this mean, and where will you fit in? How does this affect you? Granted, almost anybody can get a college degree, but thousands upon thousands of jobs are being lost to advances in technology or to foreign workforces. Then there are those who are prepared to work for a lot less money than any college graduate could ever imagine living on, and so the gap widens.

This is the new economic reality. It took a while to get here, but we have arrived and must now learn how get out of denial for the situation to improve. Read the news, watch TV, and listen to the economists. Where are all the optimists?

As we look for solutions in all the old places, we must now find new and creative ways to find opportunities. It is no longer such a big deal if you have a college degree, yet to most it is still a really big deal if you don't. An MBA, PhD, or double major might get you noticed, but there are plenty of paper-qualified candidates who paid dearly for these credentials and so, at best, they might get an interview.

With this new dynamic, one has to actually stop for a moment or two and seriously think about how best to tackle everyday situations. If one wants to prevail or simply avoid the relentless and inevitable disappointments, an earnest life strategy has to be formulated to find a place in the overcrowded and desperate workforce.

Even the more entrepreneurial types must face a new reality as more and more people get laid off and join the ranks of the unemployed. The Internet has provided an opportunity for people to easily start a business, to be their own boss, and to work from home, which has flooded the market with new competition, enough to dilute what once might have been a very lucrative environment, even for those with substantial human resources, education, and financial support. This phenomenon has forever changed the game. You can't just decide to go into business and expect to be successful. Everything is at stake. Careless risks and poorly implemented strategies make matters even worse. What should you do?

Stop for a moment and take a brand new look at everything. Life is different; the rules have changed and continue to do so every day.

Open your eyes to the fact that much of the available information must somehow be sorted and digested. It's not that difficult to do, but it is imperative. It is the era in which you simply *MUST READ MORE* and then emulate advantageous habits from others, in addition to what can be learned at school. It is time to reevaluate what is meant by "sharpen the sword" and "look before you leap" and to reengineer the very way in which we approach life, education, and execution. Bad ideas, bad habits and bad behavior must be avoided; the consequences are dire. Look around you. Is everyone having a good time? Learning things the hard way takes too long and is too expensive. There are no more means to make costly mistakes and start all over again because the game is now played very differently, in other words, the wise old man has left the building.

Learning street smarts has never been more important. Most of what you need to know about social interaction, business, and relationships can no longer be learned through trial and error and especially not at college, not yet anyway! You need to know how to behave in such a way that others will want to give you one of the opportunities that are out there. You can take a chance and learn things the old, traditional way on your own, or you might choose to pay careful attention to what older, more knowledgeable people are doing. Ask them why, what, and how they have used their experiences to ensure that they remain in the ranks of satisfied and grateful citizens.

From the way you speak, to the way you look, to the things you say and do, every little thing matters. Reality has changed and so enjoying a comfortable home and an enviable lifestyle cannot be taken for granted anymore. Success has been redefined! In the pages that follow, you will learn how to approach life with objectivity, common sense, and logic. S*marter* decisions and choices will be made.

Street Smart Tips

- *Good enough just isn't anymore.*
- *Common sense is a critical but much underused tool.*
- *The future is not what it used to be.*
- *No motivator will ever fix your problems for you.*
- *There are very important things in life that money will never ever be able to buy.*

Chapter Two

It All Starts And
Ends With Health

Baby Curtis was to be born on a bright sunny day in July, the day after his dad, Lance, got back from his annual fishing trip. Lance was feeling on top of the world! It seemed as if little Curtis' mom had waited for Lance to return from his trip before going into labor. What a perfect situation! Proud as can be, with the thrill of catching a twelve-foot marlin still fresh on his mind, Lance drove his wife, Melinda, to the hospital to give birth to their fourth child.

Lance had a great life, three healthy kids, a lovely and spacious home, a steady job and an adoring wife who enjoyed life as much as he did. She was a proud mother and more loving than anyone could imagine. It appeared to be a routine trip to the maternity ward for them, but no one could predict what was about to happen and how it would change their lives forever.

Little Curtis was born with a rare kidney disease and would need continuous and very expensive medical care throughout his unpredictable life. Poor little Curtis was about to turn this happy family's lives upside down and inside out in the worst possible way. Then, just when they finally learned to accept life like that and get back on their feet, both financially and emotionally, Curtis died at age four, leaving his entire family distraught, emotionally drained, in debt, and very much worse for the wear. They would all be affected for the rest of their lives.

Melinda suffered serious bouts of depression that put a strain on her relationship with Lance and her other three kids who never really did get their mom back.

Curtis' sister, Sarah, decided never to have kids when she was older. Melinda's brother, Paul, divorced his wife after just six months when he found out that there was cancer in her family out of fear that if they had children one day, they, too, might get sick.

The emotional damage caused by this unfortunate tragedy proved far too enduring for the entire family to ever have a somewhat normal life again.

Far too many kids in our world are doomed from day one to a life of discomfort or outright despair, both physically and emotionally. Even if we are only talking about the relatively small percentage of kids that you actually hear about, come into contact with, or can simply imagine, it is beyond comprehension how many kids in the world are never going to have the quality of life that you will most likely get to enjoy. Chances are that if you are reading this book, you are already privileged enough to be among those who can focus on becoming a valued member of the well-educated, well-balanced, and well-adjusted segment of the world.

It is an *extremely smart* move not to take your good health for granted.

Now, even if you are blessed enough to be born with all your limbs or body parts intact and functional, there is still a chance that one of the many organs that you need to enjoy a fulfilled life will not always be 100 percent useful to you; and one of them may fail you before you reach a ripe old age. There are so many things that can and do go wrong in the multiplex system that we call a human body that if you are considered to be a normal healthy child by any standards, *count your lucky stars again, and then again!*

As you read this book, you will begin to realize the amazing and incredible capabilities of the human body and mind and how it is imperative not to take them for granted.

If you happen to be one who is not able to take all your body parts for granted, you have might have been compensated in other ways.

The goal is to help everyone to uncover that extra special ability or drive that is typically hidden inside of us and to put it to good use. Every one of us has several untapped or half-tapped resources that can be used to accomplish way more than even our wildest dreams may allow us to imagine, starting right now.

It is a sad fact that many of us—if not most of us—as soon as we can, and if our parents and society have not already started doing this for us, will work quite hard to destroy our healthy bodies and minds. From having to breathe the not-so-clean air that we have inherited to the unhealthy food that we might be compelled to consume, to the many hours of our lives spent in harmful environments or stressful situations, we go about life with no thought given to their significance, until of course we have no choice. At times we all ignore the inevitable downside that comes from neglecting our bodies and minds. We will typically wait until it is *too late*!

Not sleeping much, eating processed or fatty foods, not exercising and not washing our hands frequently are ways in which we unwittingly act to weaken or destroy the most incredible, multifaceted system ever created. Yes, we all test our limits, and we often succeed—but at an enormous cost.

Your first day, the day that you are born, whoever you are, is arguably the one and only day in your life that you can be considered perfect, but, again, only if you are fortunate. Things can and do go wrong in the womb, or just after birth. An immeasurable part of the anxiety for expecting parents is not whether it will be a boy or a girl but whether the baby will be healthy and normal. Imagine for a moment how radically peoples' lives change when a baby is born with complications or defects. A heart, liver, kidneys, lungs, brain, ears, eyes, nose, and a stomach must all be in good working order, good enough to last for up to one hundred years of continuous use and abuse. More than two hundred bones and six hundred muscles make up the human body. If everything works as planned, you are at best off to a good start.

It is difficult to imagine that we, as intelligent human beings, do some of the things that we do, especially in today's world where ignorance is no longer a viable excuse. We can learn just about anything in just minutes on the Internet, in a library, or by simply asking others. Being unaware is no longer an acceptable explanation to justify the damage that we do to our bodies and minds. Armed with the knowledge, resources, and education available to us today, it's so scary to think that we still abandon our minds, bodies and souls and that we will not have the power or the will to stop it—that is, until it either kills us or tarnishes a significant part of who we are, forever. This almost always happens at far too young an age.

As you read through these pages, you will find ways to prevent you from falling into one of the many traps that lead many adults to a life filled with depression, fear, anxiety, misery, and regret. Everything that you will need to live a reasonably satisfying life can be unlocked (especially in our society) for you to use and to ensure a balanced and overall fulfilling journey.

Sure, you can wait until you are a little older and be one of the many in line to see a therapist, a therapist who might possibly also need a therapist, or you can prevent that incredible disruption in life by taking a few ideas from this book, ideas from real life, and ideas from older folks. Or you might simply revisit the good ideas that are already brewing in your very own mind, the ones that make sense and, if implemented, will work well for you.

Even when it is logical and obvious, we still choose to do things the tough way, or we simply put them off for a while because perhaps we are constantly living in a fatigued state. I can assure you that everything you do that requires significant physical energy will become more and more difficult year by year. Today is the day that it will be the easiest; tomorrow might still be fine, but down the road, you will likely lack the energy that is required to do something momentous and will once again put it off, only to discover that it is probably never really going to happen. This is exactly how regrets are made.

It still surprises me how some physically challenged folks still manage to accomplish far more with their lives than the many that were given the gift of a perfectly healthy mind and body. Many people complain when they really shouldn't and are therefore seldom satisfied with life's bounty. Anything requiring minimal exertion takes too much effort, and then it's one excuse after another that leads to a wasted body and mind.

Granted, not everyone in the world has been given the same tremendous potential. But even if you have just a little, and I believe that you do, you can choose not to waste it.

What we ultimately do with our unique potential is up to us.

Street Smart Tips

- *Be aware of what and how much of anything you put inside your body.*
- *Be concerned about what you feed your mind (garbage in equals garbage out). What you have learned is all you have to offer.*
- *You might never know how important your health is until you lose it.*

Our Bodies Are Mean Machines

John had recently received his driver's license and was driving rather carelessly down a pretty narrow street in New Hampshire. His music was very loud and he made sure that a group of young teenagers standing on the sidewalk heard him coming and going. He felt like Mr. Cool and, understandably to most experienced drivers, lost focus on his speed and especially the important details of his environment.

Suddenly a small dog with leash still attached darted into the street ten or twelve feet in front of John's car. The dog's frantic owner was a step or two behind him and, in a flash, John was faced with a horrific dilemma. He was going too fast to swerve or to stop in time and therefore simply had no choice but to run over and kill the unsuspecting little pooch. Worse yet, in this panic-stricken commotion, his fender sideswiped Mr. Freely, sending this 73-year-old retiree sprawling, while trying desperately to catch his best friend.

John's car then veered to the right and hit a lamppost, causing him to black out. When he awoke in the hospital, two uniformed policemen sent to investigate the accident stood around his bed. They informed him that in addition to a head injury, Mr. Freely had broken several bones in his frail body, including his hip. He was notably bruised from head to toe and scraped almost everywhere from hitting the rough surface of the road. After several surgeries and eventually awakening from a week-long induced coma, and after many months of rehabilitation, Mr. Freely was able to walk unassisted, but not without a noticeable limp on his left side, and of course, without his loyal companion by his side.

His most severe physical injuries healed significantly despite his age; the bruises were all gone, and the scrapes left minimal scarring.

To all, it was a miracle that he survived, as no one really considered that he might ever walk again. Mr. Feely was grateful to be alive, but he felt lost without his little dog, and this left him with an empty and sad feeling that he was unable to erase.

Witnesses came forward and made it clear that John was driving illegally fast, and because of this he lost his license for two years and his family was sued for thousands of dollars in medical expenses that took almost six years for them to pay.

One's body can be likened to a machine—not just any machine but a very, very sophisticated and elaborate machine, unlike anything ever invented, copied, or built by humans. Granted, there are some pretty mind-blowing machines in the world today: your computer, science research equipment, rockets that take people to other planets, airplanes, televisions, and turbo-charged race cars. Even the workings of a small, bedside clock radio elude most of us.

Most of us do not know, nor will we ever know, how any of these incredible modern-day marvels work. It took many years of imagination, study, collaboration, and dedication to develop and perfect the capability to manufacture some of today's sophisticated products and equipment. Despite widespread use and the abundance of affordable, elaborate technology, it should not be taken too lightly.

Now, consider your body. Take any one of the machines that I mentioned above or any one of the most complicated pieces of equipment that you might imagine existing in the future. The more demanding the better! Now, let's see. Can your contraption fix itself when it is broken? Can it last for up to one hundred years in use twenty-four hours a day, 365 days a year? Can it show compassion, take control, and really love you? No, not even almost. Absolutely not! Let's take a computer, for instance. Does it work without being plugged into something for longer than a few hours? Can it recover from a virus on its own? Can you drop it and break it and expect it to work again without your help? What if it gets completely wet, inside and out? What about operating in a very hot or dusty environment? No, no, no, and *no!*

Your body can and does go through all the above, and most of the time it comes out of it just fine. Your body does need *a little* fuel to operate effectively, and it can get sick or broken, but it is usually able to recover, even when the environment is not perfect.

However, if you constantly neglect your body, like many people do, it will eventually and tragically become unable to operate efficiently. Some bodies are built stronger than others, but the true test results are usually discovered only when it is too late and the damage is already done.

Remember this well: if and when you get seriously ill or injured, *nothing else in the world matters*, and I mean nothing. You are basically out of commission, period. Everything you really want to accomplish, even very important responsibilities or tasks that you absolutely must take care of, will either be put on hold indefinitely or simply never be realized.

What if you get so sick that you never get one hundred percent better and then eventually just wither away and die well before you are middle-aged? Imagine spending the rest of your life in a bed, using a wheelchair to get around, being hooked to a machine to be able to eat or breathe, or being heavily medicated and unable to do the day-to-day activities that most ordinary people take for granted. No hiking, swimming, running, driving, working, lifting your kids, and so forth. When you realize that you could have avoided all this by taking better care of your body or by making just one better decision when you were younger, it just won't matter anymore.

Consider to, that no matter how much money you have or can get your hands on one day, there are numerous instances where even that won't save you, not even for a day. Living with regret is no way to exist.

Your physical body is your hardware. Of course some parts can be replaced or repaired by a body mechanic (surgeon) in a few hours with a few weeks recovery, but by no means *always*. On the other hand, your well-hidden software or mind is a lot more complicated and that, too, can be broken, but it may be much more difficult and complicated to repair.

Even with incredible discipline and tenacity, it can take many, many years and untold heartache to restore it, if it can be restored at all.

Street Smart Tips

- *Being sick is really terrible. People don't appreciate this until it happens to them, and then soon after they recover, they forget just how difficult it was, until the next time.*
- *Some injuries can affect you for the rest of your life; even if they formally heal, there could be restrictions to movement or sporadic, impossible-to-ignore pain as you age.*

Hardware Maintenance

Andy and Gary, both straight A students at a very prestigious high school, got drunk one night while Gary's parents were out with their friends. They were at Gary's parents' home by themselves, knew of a way to open the liquor cabinet, and began drinking heavily and carelessly, becoming very intoxicated within a short period. The bar fridge outside wasn't even locked, and there too were various alcoholic temptations.

Gary was young, but already a regular drinker, and unknowingly had "the disease" they call alcoholism. He drank often and had no idea that he was about to go through life with a very dangerous and destructive burden. His body would crave alcohol, and so he was destined to suffer and cause suffering, not physically being able to control his body's need for alcohol. He was well on his way to dying a slow death. Would he ever enjoy life in the true sense of the concept?

Then, as drunk and foolish people often do, Gary dared Andy to do something that anyone in their right mind might consider to be dangerous; he challenged Andy to jump off the second story balcony and into the swimming pool.

Andy laughed and said that Gary was crazy, but Gary insisted that it was so much fun and that he did it all the time, no biggie! In fact, Gary said that he would go first to prove to Andy that its was a cool rush. Beer can in hand, Gary went up to the second floor balcony and jumped into the pool. He surfaced, beer intact, and laughing like a crazy man. He gestured to Andy to jump.

Andy was feeling the pressure and despite being a little buzzed, he knew that it was a foolish and dangerous idea. But since Gary had

*just done it and was yelling at him from the pool to jump, he could
not resist the pressure to be cool.*

*He stood on a small table and jumped toward the pool. In his
slightly inebriated state, his one foot barely brushed against the
railing but this threw him just a little off balance. He landed seven-
eighths in the pool and one-eighth on the brick coping. Andy lay
lifeless as blood started oozing from his right ear. He could not
move, not that day, not ever again.*

*Andy was paralyzed from his neck down and had to spend the rest
of his life in a hospital bed, unable to take care of himself in the
most basic of ways. He looked around the hospital ward and saw
that it was full of young men on one kind of life support system or
another—young, foolhardy men who had, against their better
judgment, made similar split-second decisions that left their bodies
permanently damaged.*

*Inside and out, the body has its limits. I would venture to say that it
is probably better to never have to find out exactly what yours are.*

Our bodies are *nothing* if not incredibly diverse and multifaceted. If
you stop for just a minute and think about it, on the one hand your
body has so many advanced features for getting the most out of life
and, on the flip side, so many moving parts that could fail us. It is
simply mind-blowing to think how many components we have to
rely on to keep us going, and despite the inconceivable
advancement of modern-day science and technology, we are still
unable to say that we completely understand the entire body.

When it comes to the ability to cure all ailments or prevent early
death due to sickness or catastrophic injury, we still have a long way
to go.

There are also countless people who live with all kinds of debilitating diseases and physical and mental disadvantages. We don't really know how they handle these unimaginable burdens, but somehow, they just do.

Take into account what we do know about caring for our bodies, and just ask yourself why so many people are so overwhelmingly destructive and negligent. Self-inflicted harm resulting in extreme difficulties, making life more complicated than it needs to be, is an all-too-common trait. There will be more discussion on this later in the book.

When it comes to living longer, being healthier, and feeling more fulfilled, what we put into our bodies and what we put our bodies through should be our primary focus. One tough thing that we have to learn to accept and acknowledge is that even if we do all the right things, nothing is guaranteed. In other words, from bad luck to the air that we breathe, the bacteria that find us, the lack of responsibility of others can and will all contribute to the possibility that we will live a very short or miserable life. So, we need to be careful to avoid known hazards whenever possible.

We must, however, live as if it all matters, a lot, every day. We should try hard to live responsibly and do what we can to prolong our lives and the lives of those who are dear to us. Everyone deserves a chance at living well, as do you, and to expect that we will all get old, very old. If there are others who rely on us, such as kids, spouses, parents, friends, and peers, then it is even more important that you take careful note.

There are many easy ways to care for our bodies, starting with good, basic common sense. Of course, in addition to what we eat and drink, the physical risks that we take, and the environment in which we live, discretion plays a big part. The body and the mind are connected. If the body feels bad, it will most certainly affect your state of mind. A mind gone bad will punish the body and continue to allow the bad habits to prevail. We are all armed and dangerous and can quickly destroy the very life that we are supposed to cherish.

This destruction can mostly be avoided with education, a little luck, and some guidance by someone wiser, someone who cares about you. Simply allow others to teach you how to avoid the accumulation of frustrating regrets as you age.

Street Smart Tips

- *The sooner you find out about a medical problem, the better chance you have of curing it, read up about it.*
- *Your body actually communicates with you...the language used is known as 'Aches and Pains'.*
- *Is it worse to get killed or to kill a good friend because you were negligent?*

Software Protection

Susan was a beautiful, intelligent girl who loved to dance at every opportunity. She was an honor student with dreams of becoming a veterinarian one day. One night while at a girl-friend's party, she met a young, really good-looking boy. She soon learned that he was a popular football player and had the reputation of giving a girl a good time. His parents were very wealthy, always travelling, and pretty much left him to do whatever he wanted.

Susan knew that this was the boy her parents had warned her about, but something about him attracted her, and she could not help herself from wanting to get to know him better. He seemed mildly interested but not as interested as she had hoped. A little while later, he asked her if she would like to go outside and smoke a joint with him and another couple. She immediately objected but quickly realized that if she did not, her chances of getting to know him better would quickly fade away.

So she went outside, and for the first time in her life took a hit of a joint. She coughed so much that she almost threw up, but after some attention from the other girl, the new boy gave her some wine to wash it down. She tried again until she could hold it down, and she pretended that she was alright even though she felt anything but high. Needless to say, she got quite ill that evening and had to spend a little extra time in the bathroom. The football player quickly lost interest in her and went home with another girl. Susan, however, became obsessed with being able to smoke pot like a pro, without coughing or getting sick, and after several attempts over the next few days, found that she was unable to stop thinking about it.

From that day on, it became the most important thing to her and her life became centered on getting high and hanging out with the boys and girls that smoked. Needless to say, most of her dreams and aspirations were put on hold, and they still are.

Like our bodies, our minds are fed and also have unseen moving parts. The brain is the central control system. As you grow older and if you are once again very fortunate, you will get to maintain control of your own mind. For the first few years of your life, your mind is controlled by others, and then it is gradually handed back to you, but with all kinds of ingrained beliefs and unmanaged expectations.

The babysitters, the friends, the teachers, and the society that your parents chose for you will all have had a tremendous impact on your future thinking and understanding. You will unknowingly accept many situations, some for the rest of your life because you are programmed to do so. However, at some point, you and absolutely everybody else must unravel it all and take control of your own destiny. You must be your own person and make decisions on your own, sometimes under difficult circumstances. Regardless, they will be *your* preferences and choices governed largely by the circumstances under which you are prepared to live.

This is the most difficult task as you grow up, but it is by far the most rewarding opportunity that you will ever have. You and you alone become empowered to change the course of your own life, experience the things that you might have dreamed of in the past, and make long-lasting decisions for yourself. The caveat is that you will be surrounded by countless others doing the very same thing, competing for their place on a crowded planet. However, it's worthy to consider often that many people—maybe even most people—are never allowed the freedom to choose their own course in life.

With that privilege in mind, while discovering new places, new options, and new challenges, it can become quite overwhelming for just about anybody. However, since anything is possible and somewhat predictable, let's assume that you really want to try this thing that they call "the good life."

Not everyone is automatically geared for success, and many journeys of self-discovery end up in turmoil and destruction. This can however be minimized with learning, a little good fortune, and with the support of someone experienced, someone who has shown just a little consideration toward you.

Cherish the relationships that you have with those who are prepared to help you in any way.

Street Smart Tips

- *It is sometimes difficult to know exactly how a bad influence may affect you; imagine the worst-case scenario at least once.*
- *Education lasts forever and can save your life.*
- *The more garbage that you allow to enter your mind, the more likely that some of it will spill out of your mouth, at the worst time, possibly costing you a life-altering opportunity.*

Chapter Three

Privileged, Athletic, Smart or Good Looking

Jason was born into an affluent family; he was good-looking, athletic, and always very confident. This bout of good fortune allowed him to enjoy privileges that most kids would give anything to experience. People were always in awe of him and because he was so popular, he always got to do what he wanted while others followed his every move, if only to be seen with him, let alone to get his attention for a little while.

It was not surprising when he started dating Emily, the smartest and most popular girl at school. She, too, was great-looking and always wore the latest fashions. What she lacked in personality she made up with talent and always got the lead in the school play. Because she felt entitled to the best of everything, she was sometimes guilty of being a little snobby or nasty to others for no good reason. Some said she was mean because she rarely saw her busy parents, even though "the help" provided her with every comfort at all times. You might think that people like her only exist in the movies, but too often, in many societies across the world, youngsters are exposed to a superficial lifestyle, one that they can become accustomed to from a very early age.

There were many times when the "followers" were persuaded to do homework or chores for Emily, Jason, or other kids like them because they were able to take advantage of those who believed that if they hung out with or near them, some of the good fortune would rub off. Of course, this incensed some of the other kids who recognized this purely as abuse, or were themselves sometimes publicly ridiculed by the "royal few" because they did not fall for all the hype. They were referred to as geeks, losers, or idiots because they did not fit the "too-cool-for-school" stereotype. Nasty comments, talking behind backs, and showing off were a common way of life for those who felt superior. Occasionally a physical fight would break out, but the pretty boys would always find someone naïve enough to fight their battles for them, or the girls would hide behind the ability to be cruel and demeaning on social media. Cowardly behavior would almost always rear its ugly head when the bullies could not get their own way every time they felt it was their right.

Jason and Emily and some others went through high school wrapped up in their self-righteous ways until one day it became exceedingly obvious that they were nothing more than shallow, insincere bigots and had nothing of real substance to offer anyone. They both eventually showed poorly on their university acceptance tests, and after partying their way through mediocre colleges they found it difficult to launch worthwhile careers.

In the real world, no one would put up with their attitudes and lack of respect, and it wasn't long before they found out the hard way that being spoiled was a huge drawback and not that easy to overcome. It was simply too challenging to live any other way, and they constantly struggled to adjust to what others considered to be acceptable behavior in a somewhat normal environment.

It was ironic how the "geeks, losers, and idiots" seemed to land on their feet by trading a few years of "coolness" for a lifetime of "hotness."

Mean People Are Really Just Crying For Help

Being born privileged, athletic, smart, or good-looking is one of the gifts in life that you might seriously consider not taking for granted and more importantly not abusing. Needless to say, you experience constant reminders that you are healthy and strong or attractive when participating in some form of physical activity, making decisions, or just by meeting new people. School is a breeze, sports a blast and you are either admired or envied for your performance and abilities and therefore have influence over others. You might be a jock, a bombshell or a knockout, a hunk or a stud, and never be affectionately referred to as a nerd, but beware of how you behave because deep down everyone knows that nerds rule the world, especially in the most important places.

It is *extremely smart* to recognize the true value and benefit of nature's intrinsic gifts.

These privileges should also serve as a reminder that not all people are born lucky, and so with it *comes* an exciting potential to ensure that your life turns out to be pretty darn good. With unique physical abilities, you are able to challenge the limits of your body and mind and experience the psychological rush that comes with competing, winning, or even losing by a very small margin. The emotions that surface when you play a sport, nail a tough test, or get asked to the prom by the captain of the varsity team all add a few new dimensions to your life.

Those who know realize that there is no rush like it. This level of confidence is unbeatable and, sadly, only a good few actually get to appreciate this incredible gift. However, with this opportunity, you have the ability to be a positive role model and can help others to feel the same worth that you do. The ability to motivate and influence others might be considered both a curse and a blessing. If you can help others, you absolutely must consider it.

It is worthwhile to contemplate that your physical advantages, good looks, and smarts DO NOT last forever, and so a heavy reliance on them can be a very shortsighted plan. While the short-term effects are exhilarating, fun, and do open all kinds of doors, the temptation to be carefree, reckless, unkind, and insensitive is sometimes irresistible. Less emphasis on your studies or less interest in the preparation needed for a secure future, as in the stuff regular kids have to do, can come back and haunt you down the road.

Also, being egotistical, mean, or undermining the feelings of those less fortunate (which is bullying any way you look at it) can be quite tempting, but remember that in the future, not everyone you come across will be equally enamored of your skills, charm, or pleasant appearance. And you will then have to compete for their attention with everyone else, including those who were uncaringly left in your dust.

Everyone else will have had to work extra hard to compensate for their lack of nature's favoritism and might in the future be streets ahead of you in the game of life. Not to mention, some of the individuals that were belittled by the "oh so lucky ones" will now be in the driver's seat, and dismal memories of the past will not have faded that much. Be humble and kind to everyone whose path you might cross because you never know when you will meet them again. Life has proven all too often that tables do turn.

It is particularly unfortunate that not every role model is a positive one. Many kids and adults alike become extremely selfish and allow their talents and abilities go to their heads, and they actually bully or mislead others, sometimes inspiring their followers to take a destructive course. If you have been dealt a good hand, it is much better to use that hand to help others to do better themselves. After all, you will have to live in the world that you have helped to create.

Try to also remember the very sad reality that many of the kids that are envied and looked up to are facing immeasurable private struggles in their own lives. They might be able to mask it or have the resources to cover it up in such a way that that they can appear to be on top of the world at all times. Far too many of these envied types are facing pressure, insecurities, or embarrassing problems of their own. These predicaments often result in these kids becoming mean, selfish, and egotistical because the only way that they can feel better about themselves is by putting others down. Trouble at home could be overwhelming, and the only way they get any relief is to transfer their negative experiences to others. Don't assume that those who seem to have it all actually do; while you may want what they have, you would probably not want it all if you knew the truth. After all, what well-adjusted, content, or happy-go-lucky person would ever feel the need to be nasty or hurtful to others? It just doesn't add up.

If you can help to enrich or improve someone else's life, you will not only be a real hero, but you will also have the distinct pleasure of living in better surroundings.

Street Smart Tips

- *Help others to succeed; this will automatically develop much-needed leadership skills for your future.*
- *Teach someone a new skill or an outlook; life has a way of giving back when you least expect it.*
- *Be humble and be unexpectedly nice to someone regardless of your position in the world, and more especially theirs.*

Chapter Four

The Impressions That You Make

Mr. Boston found himself unemployed due to an unexpected merger at his firm. Surprisingly, he was one of the first to be let go despite his credentials. Quite confident of replacing his job, he went on a few interviews and found it odd that he was not hired on the spot. Weeks went by and interview after interview ended the same way. "We will let you know, Mr. Boston," he was told repeatedly.

The truth is that despite is qualifications, nobody did let him know, and he remained unemployed for several months, resulting in the loss of his home to the bank and thus forcing him to endure unimaginable pressure in his personal life. His wife became fed up with the sudden upheaval, and she and their daughter moved in with her parents, leaving him to sort out the mess. Mr. Boston could not understand what was going on. Why had he not been able to find employment? He was not that old and brought value to most any situation in his field.

You see, the truth is that Mr. Boston had noticeable body odor and no matter how qualified he might have been for each opportunity, no one wanted to work with or around him. On top of everything, no one had the courage to tell him. Mr. Boston took a shower every day but failed to wear deodorant or dry clean the one very nice suit that he had owned for years, the one that he wore to every interview.

This is a common and often overlooked scenario and quite possibly the reason why many people lose very important opportunities in their lives.

Personal Hygiene

Even though we have all been told many times and are expected to just know, it is still surprising how some adults go through life in a complete fog about their personal appearance, not realizing the negative impact it has on their lives. Other than the obviously wrinkled and dirty clothing that people choose to wear, body odor, grimy fingernails, greasy hair, dandruff, and bad breath are some of the most common and very likely reasons that someone might be repulsed by you, despite all of your other admirable qualities. It doesn't always matter how smart, rich, or good-looking you are if you offend the people around you. Usually, it is just too embarrassing for someone to say anything to you, and so you will never really know why you have been avoided. Could you tell someone that his or her disgusting, personal hygiene issues disgusts you? It is tough, isn't it?

It is *smart* to be aware of your personal hygiene at all times.

As a course of habit, there are those who shower frequently enough but continue to wear sweat-stained clothing. A suit jacket or a shirt that has been previously sweated in but not laundered can harbor a nasty odor. If worn a few times too many just to save a buck or two at the dry cleaners, it may cost you a lot more at the end of the day. It may not smell bad to you or your close family since the lingering odor becomes familiar to them. But to others, it is nothing short of a nasty stench. If you smell bad, chances are that the person who is offended will want to avoid you at all costs, even though you will likely never really know why. How well and for how long would you tolerate having to work with or hang out with someone that simply seemed unclean?

No matter your talents or charm and even if you only smell slightly, your hygiene might be the daily topic of conversation at the water fountain. People will keep their distance, and if you feel the vibe but think that it is something else, you may feel a lot of anguish for all the wrong reasons. Your mind will play tricks on you, and perhaps you could develop a complex or feel generally unwanted.

It is of course true that some people sweat more than others and therefore need to take extra precautions to smell clean and fresh throughout the day. That's life; it could very well be you, and if you don't deal with it immediately, you may never know how much poor personal hygiene can and will hold you back.

Worse still, as a kid, there might be times when the only person with any interest in telling someone that they smell bad is a bully. This may be communicated mockingly and could be turned into something far worse and cause the person on the receiving end to retract and become so embarrassed that he or she loses self-confidence, develops a social issue, and pays for it for the rest of his or her life. So, hopefully by now, this message is loud and clear. Stay clean! Do it and no one will notice. Don't and everybody will.

Brushing your teeth, for example, is one of the many recommendations you have heard over and over again from well before you can remember. When you wake up, before you go to bed, and sometimes even during the day after a meal. What's up with that? The truth is that most everyone has little gaps between their teeth, and pieces of food get stuck in those gaps. Food could be stuck there for days and as nature would have it, it will start to rot. Guess what, it too smells bad. Equally bad is the fact that rotting food causes your teeth, which the food presses up against, to undergo chemical changes. The teeth begin to weaken and cavities are created. This is known as the never-pleasant phenomenon, tooth decay.

Most of your parents know this only too well, but strangely enough they may not explain it too well, which means you won't take it too seriously. They just demand it, and kids seldom react well to demands. Perhaps some parents are embarrassed to show their own teeth or bring too much attention to the issue because they found this out the hard way. Not taking care of your teeth leads to all types of other complications, including gum disease, root canals, tooth extractions, and other painful infections in your mouth. This information is everywhere, so read about it. It is real and if you choose to ignore it, you will most likely pay for it later. People hate going to the dentist for a reason: it hurts like hell, it's uncomfortable, and every time you go you leave with an appointment for another visit. Just take care of your teeth; they, too, have to last up to one hundred years.

How about cleaning your fingernails? Take a look at yours now. Don't even think of putting your fingers in or near your mouth. Do not touch anything around you; in fact, touch nothing until you go and wash your hands, especially if you are going to eat something. I am not suggesting germ-phobic behavior, but c'mon, this one is so logical and obvious. Get into the habit of washing your hands at every reasonable opportunity. This is a no-brainer and calls for washing your hands, at the very least, after every time you use the bathroom and before every meal.

The state of your fingernails speaks volumes about your personal hygiene. Unless you are some sort of mechanic or have a similar occupation where you come into daily contact with grease or sludge, you have NO excuse. If people can't take the time to keep their fingernails clean, then what else do they not clean very often or very well? Every time you exchange money, eat something, scratch anything, and so on, your hands and fingernails are subject to germs, bacteria, and who knows what else. When you shake someone's hand, you accept a little bit of whatever they have touched in the last few hours. Don't be paranoid; just be aware that your hands are seldom clean for too long during any given day.

So we nailed the finger thing, but just so you don't forget, and because it is important enough to possibly avoid at least a few of the common sniffles and bugs that you will catch throughout your life, I am once again bringing attention to a significant issue: wash your hands regularly!

It would also be a giant leap in the right direction if people automatically cleaned up after themselves when using public bathrooms. Sadly, it just isn't that way. Imagine you are a parent visiting a public park, a shopping mall, a stadium, or a school event, and your young son or daughter has to go *urgently*; maybe it's your elderly parent who has to deal with this waste-no-time situation.

You walk into a public restroom and the place is a disaster: pee all over the seat, dirty toilet tissue on the floor, and filth everywhere you look. This is an all-too-familiar scene. You don't want to touch anything, but you must and quickly. If you do actually have the time, you might have to flush the toilet, wash the seat with a wad of wet toilet paper, dry it well, and then use a couple of toilet seat covers, assuming there are any. Now the toilet is good enough for you to use. You get the picture. Now you're leaving the place cleaner than it was when you found it.

Being a respectable human being will always pay huge dividends.

Street Smart Tips

- *Be a decent human being because how you act is who you are, even if no one else sees you.*
- *If you don't care about other people, they won't care about you, and it won't always be OK.*
- *Carelessly spreading germs means that one day someone that you really care about will catch them and get sick, maybe very sick.*

Other Significant Patterns

Some other very important factors that we allow to influence our lives are often overlooked by us, but they do make significant impressions on others throughout our day-to-day activities.

Let's look at something as commonplace as table manners, for instance. When we eat alone or among close family members at home, it is understandable to be less concerned about how we eat. We often behave in such a way that we would never dream of duplicating it in front of others. Not to be too graphic, but we often do things when alone that would simply disgust others or cause them to have a poor impression of us. Often, we learn this behavior from watching our relatives, parents, or older siblings and then, unfortunately, we go outside the home and behave offensively without really knowing any better.

Poor manners are a reflection on you and your family because it is generally assumed that your parents would teach you to eat properly around others. When the opportunity arises, say, when you are in a nice restaurant or at an important function, simply take note of how elegantly some people conduct themselves during a meal. It is not to say that you must be elegant at all times, but it is good to know when the appropriate occasion presents itself. A very important gathering, a job interview, or the first meeting with your fiancé's parents might typically involve a meal together. Your table manners will no doubt create a lasting impression, and it may also create assumptions regarding your overall character and reputation. There are too many dos and don'ts to mention, but enough of them are unmistakably apparent at many tables. So, what to do and specifically what not to do can easily be learned by simply watching others.

The first impressions that you make on others will usually influence your life in all areas. Your flexibility to conduct yourself in a situation-appropriate manner will likely improve your opportunities, often making you a person with whom others will want to be associated.

It is true that we are all adversely influenced by our lack of familiarity in certain areas, but we can rise above them. No matter our challenges or handicaps, we can overcome them all with a *basic level of awareness* of our surroundings. Seek out the characteristics that set aside the ordinary folks from the extraordinary. Emulate good behavior where it is obviously impressive and abundantly used, and then set a new standard for the way in which you want your own life to unfold. There is no harm in impressing those with whom you spend your time.

It is not that complicated and typically requires nothing more than a little self-respect, self-control, and self-motivation. After all, you are doing this for yourself, so until you are satisfied with your own achievements, you can't really be of much support to anyone else, especially those who matter and eventually will come to rely on you.

Your favorite and most influential person in the world can be you, if and only if, you decide to allow it.

Street Smart Tips

- *How you conduct yourself in company is a testament to your level of education.*
- *If you have bad table manners, it is a poor reflection on your intelligence because it is something that is so easy to learn.*
- *People absolutely do judge books by their covers. What does your cover tell others?*

Chapter Five
Obsession

It was seven o'clock on a Thursday morning about twelve years after George, then fourteen, took his first drink to be cool with the guys, and now he was totally freaking out. After years of heavy 'teenage drinking' his body desperately needed alcohol and there was none to be found. He had finished everything in his apartment the night before and, as per usual, passed out on the living room floor, TV blaring and lights still on in every room.

He neglected to feed his dog, for the second time that week, and when he awoke the next day, he realized that he had not closed the living room window facing the street. This was just another in a series of lucky escapes from harm or dire consequences. He frantically searched every cupboard in his apartment, just in case there was some alcohol somewhere, even though he was quite sure that the empty bottles on the floor were pretty much it. He stumbled into the bathroom and suddenly it hit him; the aftershave in the cabinet had alcohol in it as did the cold and flu medicine.

Without further thought, he opened both bottles and downed the contents of one. It was hard to hold down and tasted terrible, but he just had to have it. His body told him so. He threw up into the sink and then finished what was left in the second bottle. This time he managed to hold it down and believed for a moment that he actually felt better.

He got dressed and went to work. Almost everyone at the office thought that George looked pale. He insisted that he was fine and went to lunch early that day. The bar was not yet open, but the bartender knew him well and let him in. It was just a matter of time before he could no longer hide his addiction. Without getting the help he desperately needed, George would likely soon be either dead or living a life of hell.

George's story is not that unique; and as is more typical today than ever before, he found comfort in the fact that other people had similar problems. He met many addicts in the every bar he visited. Some were in denial; some were "really" planning on quitting soon; and some accepted that they would just keep drinking excessively until the day they would die. What the addicts had in common was that whenever they heard someone else's sob story, (and the worse they were doing in their lives), the better it made them feel about themselves. And so George relied on their pathetic and tragic stories as a measure to justify his own way of life. After all, he still had a job, a place to live, and a car, although it did not currently run. George felt that others were in significantly poorer condition than he was, so there was no need to be that concerned, yet.

This does not seem like the *smartest* way to view the situation, does it?

Although alcoholism is by far the most widely discussed addiction, it is by no means the only substance or activity that is abused until it becomes impossible to function normally without it. Because alcohol is legal and freely available to almost anyone, we see more addicts out in the open and the abuse right in front of our eyes. It is therefore often overlooked and accepted by all until it becomes an obvious problem, meaning that it has become serious enough where medical help has to be sought or people are going to get seriously hurt.

Obsessive eating, spending, making excuses, taking pills, watching TV, telling lies, sex, gambling, and cheating are all familiar examples of potentially very bad habits that can lead to the upheaval of one's personal life, family relationships, and friendships. No matter how educated, wealthy, or prominent of a person you might become, abusing any of the above can easily overshadow the good that you will do or might have done in your life. If you are a prominent judge, banker, or politician with an exposed addiction, you will likely be known or remembered for the addiction and the embarrassment it caused rather than your good work or the countless hours that you have dedicated to your profession. Even if you are lucky enough to live through it and come out the other side, your life might have changed forever, and the so called good life you led could now simply become a mere existence, with the challenge now being to simply get through the day.

If you have yet to be fully exposed, you might be considered elusive or odd because your uncharacteristic behavior will be unfamiliar to those who know you best. Your own family members might be naïve as to the reason that you are acting differently and then instinctively distance themselves from you because you have now become less approachable than before. Because of their love and admiration for you, they will not automatically assume the worst and will probably blame your behavior on your workload or stressful responsibilities. They will not have the insight required to step in to try and help you, which is arguably the most important thing you need at the time: help from someone who really cares about you.

Why paint this picture? Well, when your dependence is eventually uncovered, besides the possibility of living as an unwell or unstable person for the rest of your life, you can no longer expect to be unconditionally trusted, respected, or honored by those who once looked up to you. You will now be perceived as weak and a potential liability, and at the slightest whim, the typical expectation is that you are on the verge of a relapse. This new perception of you could follow you everywhere. You might have dug a hole so deep that no matter what you do to remedy the situation, you will forever carry a blemish on your record and even those who really do care about you will always be on guard, forever afraid that you might just put them through a similar *hell* again (see *reputation* later in this book). You might have to find new friends and acquaintances and, equally disappointing, a new set of standards by which you will have to live. It is not uncommon at this stage for you to make or find a new family, too.

No one ever expects to become addicted to anything, and he or she is always surprised when they do, despite knowing beforehand that it was a familiarly destructive poison that they were ingesting.

Street Smart Tips

- *When you spend a significant time doing any one thing, you give up the opportunity to do something else, perhaps far more important.*
- *If you continuously talk about yourself, show off or steal all the attention, you will ensure that you have no friends.*
- *Anything that is continuously on your mind is controlling you... seek help.*

Cravings

On a broader scale, it is interesting to ponder how humans are arguably the most intelligent and capable creatures on the planet. Still, there are some unbelievable facts about the very same humans that boggle the mind. While men and women have through the ages invented the most incredibly advanced products, provided the most elaborate theories, and then developed mesmerizing life-altering skills and capabilities way beyond most everyone's comprehension, some important and interesting observations stand out.

Unlike most creatures, a human cannot survive after birth without the direct support of another human being. A newborn is totally incapable of survival if left alone for just one or two days. After years of feeding, nurturing, and physical protection, little humans then continue to be emotionally dependant on others and cannot function without some sort of constant validation. Humans are just as frail as they are resilient.

A human can build a skyscraper, a rocket, or a bridge and transplant a heart or cure a disease, but at the same time be completely helpless to the point of incapacity when it comes to self-control or a reliance on others.

The toughest business man or woman who will ruthlessly crush a competitor or cause the demise of another person's personal life is often unable to control self-destructive behaviors or will demonstrate an inability to keep another human interested in him or her long enough to provide the most basic love and affection.

Despite coaching, training, or physiological help, some of the world's most admired people suffer through untold misery and desperation because they are not wired to be able to manage all aspects of their lives. Their desire to dominate some areas or to attain immeasurable success comes at an enormous expense, sometimes to their health or important relationships. It is an art to be able to balance one's life with *enough* of what one needs and *enough* of what one wants to maintain a healthy and long-lasting lifestyle.

So many people have an insatiable desire to have way more of something than is necessary, and it is this craving that sometimes causes the lack of judgment and the inability to control their lives in other equally important areas. The inability to say no to the allure of food, drugs, or reckless behavior has taken many a prodigy down, never to be able to get up and get back in the game.

Ironically, the almighty human can be overcome by the yearning for something he or she cannot have. It is most often the things that money cannot buy that are the most desired, or the inability to avoid that which will render you helpless that will turn a powerful person into a helpless victim.

Even more surprising is that, unlike our furry friends, humans are also guilty of doing the things that they know will hurt them and, even after having had a very bad experience; they will often repeat the very same behavior with the same detrimental results. Go figure.

A Bit About Medicine

The medicine that we most frequently come across is typically used to relieve pain and the discomfort caused by a sick body or mind. Actual medicine, itself is anything but good for you. The way medicine typically works is that it either masks the pain you are feeling by numbing your nerve endings or, in some cases, destroys the root of the problem by poisoning the bad cells or bacteria in your body that are causing you to be sick.

Your body does, however, have many of its own mechanisms to rid itself of unwanted matter or interference. Use your imagination and you will realize that once again, your body is an incredible machine. So, the point is that if whatever it is that you are experiencing is *unbearable or dangerous* then medicine should be considered. It is at best a short-term solution. If you take any medicine without really being sick or without the express recommendation of a competent doctor, chances are it will be worse for you than the ailment it is meant to relieve. When people die from an overdose, it is because they either took too much of a medicine for their body to tolerate, or they mixed different medicines and the reaction proved to be fatal. Of course, they never get to find out because they are already dead.

Let's face it. No one other than a pharmacist really knows what goes into medicine, and even then, after it is approved by some big government agency, such as the FDA, it is discovered years later that the medicine you were prescribed for your heart or back is really bad for your kidney or liver. Look at all the disclaimers on medicines today; every side effect is disclosed. These are serious and many state that what you are taking for a particular ailment may well cause many other problems and may even kill you. So, why on earth would any intelligent person take any laboratory-made medicine unless it was absolutely necessary? Even so-called legal drugs can be addictive. It is reported that prescribed painkillers are involved in the death of more people in the United States than both heroin and cocaine combined.

Processing prescription medicine is an unimaginably huge commercial entity that is sometimes guilty of neglect or deception, usually for financial gain, while promoting the use of a particular drug. Think very carefully before you subject yourself to a course of chemicals that may have unknown side effects for you because they do not necessarily affect all people the same way. Imagine owning a business that provides expensive addictive drugs to people who cannot stop taking them, even if they desperately want to. Am I the only one who thinks this is a questionable situation?

OK, you know that we absolutely have to go here. Another familiar word for *medicine* is *drugs*. Medicines or drugs are made up of supposedly carefully measured amounts of different chemical compounds. Mixed incorrectly, they could be fatal. Taken incorrectly, they could yield the same results. Buying drugs on the street—drugs that are made in an underground, illegal, and untraceable lab—or from a "friend" is one sure way to risk your life and bring the worst possible nightmare home to your family.

Getting hooked on any laboratory-made drug is so serious that the chances of ever having a normal life afterward are very slim. You always remain affected, even if it's just always on your mind as something you have to avoid at all costs. Over-the-counter drugs are sometimes just milder forms of prescription drugs, but it is possible to abuse any drug. So, don't believe that because you can purchase something at the drugstore it is harmless.

Every human is made a little differently so each of us continues to change as we age. For this reason, we can react to certain substances in an unpredictable way, possibly developing new allergies as an example, or just by having a negative reaction to certain substances when using them for the first time. Some people react to medicines in ways that others don't. In fact, just like medicines, illegal drugs are potentially deadly if abused or ingested without the proper direction of a trained doctor or pharmacist.

Every time you put chemicals into your body, you run the risk of a bad reaction, whether immediate, deferred, or not noticed until one day in the future when the cumulative effects have caused permanent damage.

Why the danger? Well, it's because of how drugs can make you feel, and this, of course, is a whole other story. Addiction is a very scary world. Your body, once exposed, may become addicted and then it physically craves the chemical and cannot do without it, no matter how hard you, your parents, friends, or doctors try to save you. It is very often beyond the resistance of a human body and mind, and the more you use it, the deeper the addiction becomes.

The drugs can replace natural chemicals made by neurons in your body and even destroy them, making you completely dependent on the so-called replacement. You can lose all control and then stop at nothing to get more of the drug into your body. There are horrific stories about what people will do for a fix. That is why it is common for evil people to get girls hooked on hard drugs so that they have complete control over them, knowing that they will do anything for a shot in the arm, and I mean anything.

Think of being high on chemicals as being able to fly. I am sure that it feels great soaring through the air, free as a bird, but only until it wears off and then you fall, crashing to the ground. You are bruised and battered, and the only way to feel better is to fly again. And until you do, you will just lie there and agonize in the worst possible way. Then, you get another dose and fly again. Only this time, you need more of the very expensive drug to stay up in the air, and if you don't get it, you come crashing down again, even harder, until you stay down for good.

Think about why so few people risk the exhilarating opportunity to skydive. I am sure that people believe that it is euphoric and incredibly fun, but they still won't try it because they can't help thinking that something will go wrong. Look at drug use the same way. What if you jump once, the parachute opens, and all ends well, but you just don't really want to jump anymore because it was a little scary. But you are forced to, and you are continuously pushed out of the plane over and over again. Each time you believe that your parachute will open, but there is always a slight chance that it won't, and you can't help thinking about what will happen. The odds that your chute will fail increase every time you take the plunge; but you can't stop and are just not sure when it's going to happen. Are you still having fun?

As important, even if you are not physically hooked, there is the psychological dependency that drugs may trigger. For some with a difficult to manage lifestyle or a series of stressful circumstances, the belief is that drugs can help. Rest assured that there can be an emotional dependency that is just as strong as the physical dependency, and this grip can be just as strong. It might never be beaten; life will be too difficult without medication. Game over.

In conclusion, all drugs or medicines, whether illegal or not, are extremely dangerous. When they are used under the wrong circumstances, they can rob you of a good, quality life. Yet, intelligent human beings with adequate knowledge will continue to mix drugs and then add alcohol just to improve the high. It is an incredibly scary and hard-to-understand phenomenon. Any questions?

Street Smart Tips

- *Medicine is big business; they are counting on your weaknesses.*
- *A drug dealer's mission is to make you a repeat customer, until you die.*
- *If you don't have any money and need drugs badly, try to imagine the extent of what one might do.*
- *Everyone that is strung out on drugs is someone's desperate child, and many will never recover, no matter what their parents are prepared or able to do.*

Chapter Six

Going Overboard

Miriam was always the life of the party and she appeared to have the energy of a hurricane. She never really relaxed in the true sense of the word and would go for hours and hours. She was always either popping or sipping something. She took energy supplements just to help her stay alert, but then she would eventually crash, sleeping for up to fourteen hours at a time. Since she really hated missing anything, when she awoke she was back at it again, trying to do everything to get the scoop on everything. She didn't know it, but this caused her body more than the usual safe amount of stress.

During any given week, she would stay awake half the night, experimenting with new concoctions to keep her going until she became too tired to function and make it into work the next day. On occasion she would swagger in, but it was evident that she could hardly perform as expected. She kept this up for days on end until she eventually succumbed to her revitalization crash in the lunch room and then had to go home sick, all while making some far-fetched excuse that usually came out all wrong. This obviously stirred suspicion among her co-workers, which eventually found its way to her supervisor.

Consequently, Miriam developed an anxiety disorder and had to be medicated on a regular basis. It was the exact opposite "medicine" to that which she was accustomed to taking before. So, up and down she went trying to create a balance, until she became too messed up and afraid to stop taking the medicine prescribed by the psychiatrist. She soon became reclusive and withdrawn. She was very unhappy and could not make any real connections to people, so no more friends and no more fun until she conquered this hurdle.

Her energetic and carefree way of life and her childhood dreams of becoming a mother and raising a family one day were put on hold, indefinitely.

Fast forward, Miriam is now fifty-eight years old and never did completely overcome her fears and anxiety; she lives alone with her cats, and works long hours in a neighborhood flower shop for a meager hourly wage. She is not all that outgoing and so typically finds peace in arranging flowers in the back room throughout the day—that is, until her mind wanders off as it often does, imagining what could have been.

As previously mentioned, and worthy of repeating, your body and mind are beyond believable and nothing short of astonishing. We could spend the rest of our lives studying the capabilities of our beings and still leave a lot to be discovered. Although we continue to discover new things every day, we have only scratched the surface.

Having said that, what we do know so far is that there are limitations, requirements, and recommendations to maintain our bodies and minds.

If you are fortunate enough to find and maintain your equilibrium and can pace yourself accordingly, it is believed that you will live longer, healthier, and perhaps get to enjoy an easier journey than most. People who understand the ill effects of overindulgence but then choose to ignore the warnings are nothing short of foolish; a blatant disregard of warnings is not recommended under any circumstances.

Granted, sometimes it is imperative to push a little harder than usual in order to achieve certain goals, but the risks involved certainly need to be weighed against the rewards. Understanding the limitations of the human body can sometimes be more important than discovering its full potential.

Much like any high-performance machine, automobile, or computer system, we too need gears and various operating modes to facilitate cruising rather than staying stuck in high gear throughout the day. The lack of a low gear will no doubt lead to unhealthy stress and serious wear and tear on our bodies. If we cannot monitor ourselves well enough and constantly allow pressure or abuse to overcome our bodies and minds, our lives will be either cut short, or we will simply *be forced* into rest mode, otherwise known as too sick to function normally.

Unlike automobiles, we do not have an external revolution counter attached to our foreheads to tell us that we are now operating in the red zone and should change gears. Some of us do, however, have something similar called parents and teachers, but we all know that *they seldom know what they are talking about anyway*, so we choose to ignore them. We ultimately have to rely upon common sense (that's sometimes a tough one) or a chest pain or dizzy spell to know when to change gears in order to relieve the tension or stress that we are, voluntarily or not, faced with on any given day. And no, it is not alcohol or drugs that will help. You cannot treat symptoms, so getting enough rest, eating healthy, and maintaining a sensibly balanced lifestyle will do us the most good.

So many have simply lost control of their own lives and are either dead young or remain bedridden, wishing that they did not push themselves so hard. Getting to the point of no return usually takes a lot of determination and typically results in unenviable predicaments. The phrase "too late" is one of the saddest and is very often associated with the fact that people ignored warnings or disregarded obvious signs, despite knowing that the risks would be intolerable, if not deadly.

It is important to look at the big picture; there are highly recommended self improvement methods to help based on research and experience. Too much deviation or lack of attention to these common sense findings could lead to regret and sorrow.

While beyond amazing, a human body does have limitations, so be *smart* enough to know yours well and adjust accordingly.

Street Smart Tips

- *Stress is commonly known as the silent killer.*
- *Your body needs rest or sleep to operate efficiently; tired people get sick more often.*
- *Just because you can't see the damage does not mean that you won't be affected, and there is no turning back when you do.*

Bad Habits—Making Excuses

We all—and I mean all of us—have bad habits to go along with our good ones. Some are bad for us, some are bad for others, and some are bad for everyone. As caring humans, we mostly try not to let our bad habits affect everyone else but, unfortunately, without thinking about it too much, most of our bad habits do affect a few people. Ironically, it's most often those who really love and care about us the most.

You see, our bad habits typically hurt or disappoint those who are frequently around us. There is smoking, drinking, eating, cussing, spitting, gambling, lying, watching TV all day, taking advantage, bullying, cheating, stealing, and so forth, and of course there is always the justification of why we cannot stop the behavior.

Specifically, one bad habit encompasses and affects all the other bad habits: making excuses. Although we are quite aware that our excesses (a.k.a. abuse) are detrimental and often hurt others, we continue our behavior regardless. Creating viable excuses for our actions is the root of why we can't—or say that we don't really want to—stop our most destructive behaviors.

If we were to stop making excuses for our rotten actions and take a hard look at the negative effects, the worst habits would eventually die. Once the excuse or the justification for the continuous indulgence is gone, it becomes apparent that it is illogical to behave in such a way, and we would most likely stop the madness. After all, why would any logical, intelligent, and sane person do anything to hurt himself or herself, regardless of the risk to others, if he or she could actually help it?

We are, after all, *the only ones* who can stop or start our behavior. Usually when someone else has to interfere or become involved in our ability to steer our destiny, we are already in big trouble, and life is going to be far from a breeze. In the future, despite successful rehabilitation, it might be impossible to go back to the exact way it was.

So, if you can crush the number one problem, which is thinking that it is okay to make excuses for irrational behavior, then your approach to all the other potentially dangerous activities can be better managed through the use of your own common sense. We all have common sense, but often choose not to use it. I am not here to tell you not to ever do any of the relaxing, goofy, risky, exciting, well-marketed, and financially lucrative activities that are a part of our society, but, like it or not, I am urging *you to think about all the possible consequences* for at least a few seconds before you act, especially when your self-control is in question or abusive behavior is about to come into play, in fact, when any need for moderation proves to be too challenging.

Age plays a very important part in one's addictive tendencies; the younger you are, the less you understand the complex dangers that exist, and the more ferociously our *developing body and mind* can be attacked and become more permanently affected. Unfortunately, many kids are subject to adult-orientated literature and activities at far too young an age, and the ill effects often prove to be eternally devastating.

Sure, we can blame our parents, which is all too often right on the mark, but unless they can be called upon to fix the mess that they allowed us to get ourselves into, it is best to recognize as soon as possible that you are going to have to sort it out on your own, sooner or later. On the other hand, try and learn from those who do seem to have it together (even though life will teach you that no one really has it *all* figured out). Even so, learning as much good as you can from the right people is by far your most realistic chance at success today.

Generally speaking, no one person can really teach you how to completely stand on your own two feet in college, at home, or at the office, but people leave clues everywhere that can help and influence you. At the end of the day, you will always be held accountable for your decisions that will affect your life, one way or another.

Life is filled with *deep ends* and, sooner or later, you are going to land up in one. It is, therefore, better to have at least some thought about it first, or at least acknowledge the warnings. The preparation for tomorrow's challenges should not be flippantly brushed off by foolish egos or ignorant bouts of denial. Do you really want to have to learn how to swim the very first time you fall overboard on a transatlantic cruise through rough seas?

So, seriously consider minimizing or avoiding any destructive habits that could lead to addiction and then a lifetime of struggle. It is strongly advised, if it becomes evident that all is not well-balanced in your own life, to tap into the many resources available, including well-trained professionals. Or, browse through any of the many self-help books available almost everywhere.

When you first find that you cannot control your self-destructive habits and you then become used to it, the despair becomes your new reality. It then becomes worse; perhaps even a lot worse, before you realize that substantial help is required.

Don't be too embarrassed to come forward and ask for help because, after all, we do live in a world where succumbing to the many enticing temptations is not only assumed but almost expected. People are people, and once in a while they find themselves in a little trouble. Even though there are those that do ask for help, not everyone escapes from all their dangerous encounters; many are left with dreadful consequences and are unable to stop until it is too late.

Do not be afraid to seek help for the sake of what "everyone might think." There are many dedicated and well-trained professionals who have made it their life's work to ensure kids do not waste away their lives. If you continue to try and justify or deny the fact that you are in serious trouble and choose not to get help, it might already be obvious to others, but you will likely be brushed aside as someone else's problem and, unfortunately, not get the help you need.

Regardless of the actual addiction, once it has begun its adverse effects on your development, it must be stopped in its tracks. The first line of defense is always to acknowledge that you have a problem with a root cause and that the euphoria, withdrawals, and obsession that you experience are just the symptoms. Symptoms cannot typically be effectively treated; they are usually just covered up or temporarily masked by prescription drugs. There are drugs to get you off drugs. Can you see a pattern here?

If you do believe that your life is in danger of imploding, it is perfectly reasonable and understandable that you may not be able to fix it alone. There is no shame in asking someone to help you put your life back on track, should some bad habit have come knocking on the door and overstayed its welcome. It does not always have to be formal help, as long as you first acknowledge the problem and talk to someone—anyone. Each small step in the right direction is critically important in solving the issue.

After all, if you are the one who makes the decision to take the first step and seek and accept help from another person, a book, or a related resource, then you can credit yourself as the *primary* reason for your well-being and your health improving—and even a little better is always better. Our own pattern of behavior is the ultimate foundation for every success or failure that we experience, drug related or not.

Making excuses for destructive habits is like trying to put a fire out with gasoline.

Street Smart Tips

- *There are things that simply cannot be done for you. Figure them out as soon as possible.*
- *Self-motivation is the secret sauce to all long-lasting, successful endeavors. There is no substitute.*
- *Seek to clearly understand the difference between accepting what you cannot change and changing what you cannot accept.*

Moderation

Moderation is the key, sound familiar? Too much of anything is considered bad, no matter what it is. Since you are completely accountable for what you do, you can really do whatever you want to, but just make sure that it is in moderation, enough not to hurt yourself and especially not anyone else. Being irresponsible is not only risky to your own physical health, but it can also lead to the injury or death of others around you. Seriously, it *can* happen to you.

Consider what would happen if you hit and kill someone else's child with your car because you were too wasted to drive safely—but did so anyway. Perhaps you are the one to introduce another kid to drugs from which they may never escape addiction. Granted, you might get away with it many times until the one time that you don't, but all the wishing in the world will NOT turn back the clock. If you don't feel this, then visit the paraplegic ward at any hospital. Chances are you will see someone your own age, whose life is basically over because they simply ran out of luck; maybe it was the very first time they tempted fate, but probably not.

Generally, when people get hurt or killed by accident, it's only an accident for the victim, the one that was minding his or her own business. When the victim was struck and paralyzed by an impaired driver, the impaired driver did not have an accident; rather, the impaired driver was out looking for trouble and found it. If you cannot stop destructive behavior (whatever it), get help right away, before you have to hear those scary little words, "It's just too late!"

Think carefully about the perils of disproportionate use of anything, even something as innocent as chocolate, soda, candy, or fried foods. Also consider the risks of being overemotional, too much in love, or simply just too nice to a point where people take advantage of you. Too much of a good thing is not a good thing anymore!

Street Smart Tips

- *Almost anything that you have heard of can happen to you.*
- *You cannot turn back the clock and wish that it did not happen; you can go to sleep, drink too much, or take drugs to forget, but if and when you come to, it will still have happened.*
- *Lack of self-control will eventually ensure that you get to taste hospital food.*
- *Do what you really love to do in moderation, so you don't have to give it up!*

Chapter Seven

Taking The Easy Way Out

Darryl had not completed his homework and his book review was due the very next day. He would have to stay up all night to finish reading the book and then write a review to hand in to his teacher. It counted toward a fair portion of his final grade, but he got distracted once again and, consequently, put it off until it was just not going to happen. He could have stayed up all night, but he found out about an opportunity to buy summary notes and quickly decided that it would now be an unnecessary waste of his time to read the book.

He handed in his work on time and felt somewhat relieved. A few days later, he got his grade back. The teacher gave him a "C." He failed to realize that his teacher would recognize the fact that the work was not his own since he was of course not the first student to try this trick. He was somewhat disappointed by his grade and knew that his parents would be very upset and probably punish him, but it wouldn't be anything that he couldn't handle. Regardless, deep down inside, he knew that it was just what he deserved, so he accepted it knowingly and moved on. His other grades were quite good, so his aggregate score was only somewhat affected. It was nothing to be too concerned about.

A few years later, Darryl, now an established building contractor, was faced with yet another time-related dilemma. Once again, he knew of a shortcut and remembered well that there was always an easy way out, so he went ahead and built a house using readily available shorter wall braces than what was required by the city's planning division. The correct braces were accessible, but they would take an extra week to arrive and would most likely make him *late completing the job. He would be penalized and lose $8,000. So, he found a way to cover up using the shorter braces, finished building the house on time, and was paid as promised.*

Three years later, he received a subpoena to go to court and face criminal charges because a wall in the bedroom of the house that he built collapsed and injured two of the family's children during a mild earthquake. A subsequent investigation revealed that he never did use the correct materials and that he was now being held liable for the repair of the house; he was also being held accountable for the injuries sustained by the kids. He was found guilty and consequently fined $35,000 in addition to being sentenced to four years in prison. Furthermore, he had to pay another licensed builder to fix the house to code, an additional $19,000.

His taking the easy way out cost him significantly more than the initial $8, 000. He of course lost his license to build homes, restricting his ability to earn a living as a contractor. After his release from prison, and very much in debt, Darryl can now be found at the racetrack almost every day, drink in hand, trying desperately to make a quick buck on the horses. He has yet to win anything substantial, another four years later!

A few different ways can be found to do almost anything. Most people find that there is an easy way and the harder way, which is usually more time consuming and costlier. In most cases, the harder way is the safer, longer lasting, and obviously the correct way, which in Darryl's case was mandated by expensive permits and by the annoying scrutiny of trained inspectors. The easy way, on the other hand, usually takes the least amount of time possible but often leads to the need to have another try or to do it another way later on.

The logical way is to take the necessary time, follow the instructions, lay the foundation, sow the seeds, monitor the progress, and then reap the rewards for a long, long time thereafter. This goes for your education, building relationships, and many other overlooked facets of life. Quality takes time; it is a universal truth. Many sayings allude to this idea such as haste makes waste, look before you leap, a stitch in time saves nine, and so on.

There is typically no such thing as free education, so you could choose to spend minimal time or money upfront and possibly have to do it over and over again at greater cost. So, consider paying your dues up front (with education, determination, and honesty), and you'll do it only once, the right way, the very first time. There are two price options: pay a little more now and just do it once, or go for the lesser amount with the possibility of the cost being multiplied later. The headaches associated with the latter are always free.

Our society and the way in which we live puts us under a lot of pressure to perform quickly, which often leads to the temptation of taking chances and shortcuts that might come back to haunt us. It is important to reflect on the best and most reliable way to tackle a project, especially when it takes the interests of others into account. It is one thing acting recklessly and hurting yourself, but when your actions put the lives or well-being of others in jeopardy; it becomes a far more serious matter. Many government-controlled regulatory agencies are there to make sure that buildings are built to code, food is cooked to the right temperature, information is taught correctly, and regulations are followed, all of which ensures the safety of the general public.

While it is always possible to cheat, deceive, or take shortcuts, the consequences can be overwhelming for at least one of the parties involved. It is a good idea to carefully weigh the risks of completing a task halfhearted or short of the requirements. While you might get away with it a few times, the habit will inevitably catch up to you one day, quite possibly causing you an unmanageable world of regret. What might being able to sleep soundly in your own comfortable bed every night be worth to you? Can you put a price on it?

Keep in mind that an average lifetime provides more than enough time and opportunity to do what must be done correctly, as well as plenty occasions to derive pleasure from the fruits of your labor.

Rather than opt for the instant but often temporary gratification, consider the *smarter* alternative of taking the time to build something worthwhile and permanent.

Street Smart Tips

- *Laziness is a self afflicted disease.*
- *Those that go the extra mile will always be ahead of you in everything.*
- *Your mind and your body can tolerate much, much more than you can imagine.*

Risks, Rewards, And Consequences

For every action, there is a reaction. Does that sound familiar? When you make decisions—and we all do every day, some without thought, some moderate, and some very difficult—as mentioned in this book before, it is a good idea to take a few extra seconds to think about *all* the possible outcomes of the decision you are about to make.

This might just be the single most important lesson in this book. An extra few seconds of contemplation might save you a few years of trying to turn back the clock. (Turning back the clock has yet to be achieved, and the odds of this happening in the near future don't look very good either.)

Our decisions can be broken down into two categories: those with short-term consequences and those with long-term consequences. Short-term decisions drive our day-in and day-out momentum and are made specifically for instant gratification or simple subconscious survival. As we react to countless little units of reasoning every day, most will need very little thought because we have come to experience negligible consequences as a result. We accept the outcome without as much as a second thought; we seldom change these habits, although we can if necessary. We make quick adjustments and then move on. This is the essence of living. We wake up, and then we decide, act, adjust, decide, act, and adjust, and then we do it all over again and again, until we go to sleep.

Remember, though, that some short-term decisions can have long-lasting effects. A few simple examples are not brushing your teeth properly, not washing your hands often enough, treating someone rudely, or eating food that is not healthy. Again, for every action, there is a reaction—maybe not immediate, but nothing goes unnoticed or unpunished forever.

Long-term decisions, on the other hand, have far-reaching effects, and they shape the very pattern of the life you are prepared to accept for yourself, as well as for your family, associates, and friends as they come and go. One hundred years of life is a very, very short time, especially for a healthy seventy-five- or eighty-year-old. The past has flown by at an alarming rate and, unless life is unbearable, it is likely that you will want to keep living as long as possible to finish something significant that you started, to get more time with your loved ones, or to finally achieve what was once just a wild dream, and so on.

So, how you choose to live your life really does matter. Your education, the people you surround yourself with, and the paths you choose to follow will all dramatically affect the way you enjoy your one and only life. Mess it up early, and you'll get to regret it longer.

Make a few really smart choices when you are young, and you might get so much out of life that you will scream with delight when alone because you just can't believe how good it is. The very emotions that surface from deep within a human soul, the smile that only you can see, the happiness that you will thrive on, cannot be bought with cash, check, or credit card.

Don't look for any easy fix. The preparation and dedication that go into building a life of fulfillment and joy are directly dependant on the long-term commitments that you have chosen.

Consequences are not necessarily just in reference to bad outcomes because there are good and great consequences that come from good and great choices; there are no guarantees, but they're certainly a worthwhile investment in anyone's book.

If you make a decision, or if you fail to make a decision when one is needed, you will be subject to the consequences of those conditions. It's inevitable, and although the outcome may not be immediately apparent, one day when you look around (and you will), you will see that what you have created is a direct result of the risks you took and the commitments you made. The good outcomes will be obvious, and the bad ones, well, perhaps they will be even more obvious because we as humans tend to remind ourselves more often about how bad things are rather than how good things are.

We tend to take so many good things for granted, which is OK to a degree but it is the not-so-good outcomes, bred by uncalculated risks, that we are forced to accept because this is what we settled for way back then.

It is often a good dose of *street smarts* coupled with a good formal education that ensure we get the very best out of life, a life that has so much good to offer that it is an absolute shame not to take full advantage of it whenever possible.

Street Smart Tips

- *When kicking yourself, you probably deserve it.*
- *Deciding not to decide is usually not a winning strategy.*
- *Live today as if it's your last day because so far, it is.*

Clever Versus Intelligent

Whether or not some people are damned because they are not born intelligent is debatable. The mere fact that you are reading this means you have most of the tools to take control of your own destiny when it comes to this argument. Reading is the second most important component of learning, *awareness* being the first. If you can read, you can learn, and there is no limit to what's possible.

There are stories of success that you might find hard to believe, but there are many more that are easy to believe because they happen every day. Sometimes success is simply defined as not screwing up what you already have. On the other hand, the power of knowledge that is used well and the sheer drive of one human can change the world—at the very least, your world.

Not all intelligent people are clever, and not all clever people are necessarily super intelligent. Arguably, as humans, we all have enough intelligence to decide how to proceed under normal circumstances, but many very intelligent people are unable to function well because they are not able to be clever when they really need to be. Consequently, extremely intelligent people could quite easily end up living a lonely life filled with sorrow and remorse. They may be quite talented or gifted in some areas and achieve what others simply cannot, but they fail miserably trying to achieve peace in other parts of their lives. Therefore, consider that the goal in life is not to compete with others, nor to compare your own life to theirs, because not one of the so-called intelligent people out there has it all.

The safest and smartest way to compete, if you have the spirit, is to compete against the person that *you* were yesterday. Striving to be better today and looking forward to improving even more the next day is bound to provide you with the ultimate winning strategy!

Think about being the best you can be at everything you do. There are builders, teachers, nurses, scientists, and there are janitors, chefs, and gardeners, all important people but with different interests and capabilities. Every human is unique, and we need them all. What matters is your making the best use of the tools you have been given and then, if desired, acquiring additional tools along the way. No one can ask you for any more than your best, and if you can go to bed at night knowing that you gave it your best, you should find it easy to sleep and to be happy, confident and proud.

Most likely, you will be excited to continue the journey every morning when you wake up.

What we have to work with is very different from person to person, and the people you meet have a different set of parameters and unique equipment tailored to their game plan. While two people may appear to be similar and have a few of the same tools, they are typically quite different in their attitude, capabilities, and motivation because of where they have been and where they think that they want to be going. How they each decide to manage their journey is what we refer to as *life*.

For example, it is obvious that everyone has the same basic body parts. But some people have more strength, better coordination, healthier organs, different resistance to the environment, completely different levels of energy, and the list goes on and on. Then, consider one's mind. No one really knows what goes on in there, and then to complicate matters further, it doesn't stay that way for long either. You can, therefore, only really rely on the consistency of your own attitude as the actual base for success. Despite life's hardships, when people with similar attitudes get together, they can move mountains.

So, even with average intelligence, you can be very clever by learning to do the things that have been proven by others to work well. Sure you get schooled by learning from your mistakes, clever by not repeating them, and street smart by allowing other peoples' triumphs and misfortunes to teach you too. You then feed your intellect by acknowledging and accepting ultimate responsibility for your accomplishments as well as your failures.

No one is lacking in *all* the tools needed to succeed, and so focus on being the best version of you instead of trying to be like someone else. You will lose every time! Sure, you can learn a few of their good habits, adopt a similar positive attitude, and follow some of the same principles that lead them to their successes, but remember, you have no real idea what is going on in their minds and their space, nor will you truly understand their incentives and challenges, so don't spend your time chasing someone else's dreams.

You are already bright enough to have your own dreams; now try to be clever enough to put your own best foot forward! Otherwise, you might turn out to be a poor imitation of another human being rather than being an original and achieving your own goals.

It is safe to say that even the most admired people that you currently know of cannot do *everything* as well as you can!

Street Smart Tips

- *Everyone that has something you want also has something that you really don't want.*
- *Learn from other people's mistakes; it is a bargain.*
- *There is no such thing as free education.(but this is pretty close, so please read on)*
- *Goals are dreams with time limits.*

Chapter Eight

Learning The Good, The Bad, And The Truth

It was half past ten at night, and Annie was supposed to be asleep. She was just fourteen years old, and it was way past her expected bedtime. She had to be up at 6:45 a.m. the next day to get to the school bus on time.

Her parents thought that she was asleep, but Annie was still on her computer surfing the Internet because, after all, there were so many exciting things to discover. She found a website that was filled with interesting things that some unusual people do. It was mostly exciting but also a little scary because it was obviously shocking material that she would never learn at home from her parents or any of her current friends. She just could not help herself and surfed through page after page.

She learned new information about serious partying, the latest slang words, and the different kinds of trendy, cool moves that were popular among the so-called new generation. She learned about the reasons why some kids tattooed themselves, pierced their bodies, skipped school, had sex in different and unusual ways, and how and why they experimented with alcohol and different types of drugs. She also learned how to get a backstage pass to her favorite band's performance, and boy was it exciting! What she did not learn, though, was what all these kids had in common, about their family environments or some of their fears and feelings of insecurity.

She did, however, recognize that nothing she had just learned was going to be good for her in any way, but it was oh so thrilling and mystifying that she found it hard to look the other way. She had to ensure that neither her parents nor her teachers would ever find out about all the things that she now knew.

The next day her school assignment was to find out about the history of her town. She had turned on her computer, and after about three minutes of reading boring statistical information, she quickly went back to the site that was filled with far more stimulation. She soon began corresponding with a boy named Scoot and learned of a couple daring places to go and a few new things to try.

It was almost dinnertime, and she had barely started her homework. She lied to her mom and said that she felt sick and needed to go to her room and rest. While in her room, she hurriedly tried to complete her school project but without much focus, and in doing so created nothing more than a mediocre presentation. So that she could get back to the cool websites as quickly as possible, she just blew through her homework. Needless to say, her project received a "C," and her parents were surprised and, of course, very upset with her. She was then compelled to cover it up with another lie and so blamed not feeling well on her poor performance.

Her relationship with her mom gradually deteriorated as she soon became a slave to the arguably irrelevant and mind-wasting content on the Internet. The same Internet that was filled with an extensive library of interesting, useful, and informative wisdom that could help to educate her instead turned her head to mush. She went on to spend hours and hours every week on the senseless garbage that was spewed all over the many sites she visited and, after a few years, when it was time to graduate high school, she paused for a moment and realized that if she had spent just half the amount of time learning important and helpful information, her grades would have been good enough for her to get into the college of her choice.

Instead, she landed up and then eventually flunked out of a community college. She now works as a night-shift cashier at the local supermarket, which, granted, is a big step up from the prior four years of just bagging the groceries.

Because it is so easy and exciting to learn bad things, we often choose them over the good, even in good conscience. After all, most bad things are exciting, and the more taboo they are, the more we want to see, feel, and hear as much of them as we can handle. We can't seem to get enough and want it even more once we have been warned to stay away. We tell ourselves that a little of it is not too bad, but then a little turns into more and then a lot and then into a destructive pattern, which can go unrecognized and therefore untreated for many years.

This is human nature, and we are all a part of it; and it is almost believable, no matter your justification, that the bad is out there to create balance. How would you know what good was if there was no bad to compare it to?

On the flip side, there are harmful temptations that are very strong, and there are people, those who do love you along with those that don't, that will pull you toward these enticements and watch as you helplessly fail to tip the scales in your favor.

Learning to love bad ideas will most likely catch up with you in the end and certainly alter your path in life. This will in turn, create a few unwelcome detours and diversions along the way, perhaps when you least expect or need them, like when they affect relationships and opportunities in the worst possible way.

Learning good concepts, however, can also last forever and touch the lives of those around you, but in a positive and motivating way.

Most of us become parents and then teach our kids what we know or have learned along the way during our own journeys. It is common and fair, albeit uncomfortable, to state that parents teach their kids some seriously bad habits. Bad behavior is typically learned by watching what others do and that goes double for whatever you see in your own home. One might wonder if it is just too much of a challenge expecting to be able to bring up well-balanced, good kids in the world today. Confronted by the destructive habits that humans learn, in their very own homes, it makes you wonder how to avoid the threat of hopelessness in the future.

One who is burdened by bad habits will certainly experience hard times and will most likely encounter hurt and disappointment quite often. Unless you are clearly able to tell right from wrong and allow right to prevail, life will most likely teach you over and over that it is *smarter* to do the right thing the first time, even in today's cutthroat world.

Street Smart Tips

- *You can lie to others and get away with it, but if you lie to yourself, there is nowhere to escape.*
- *If you know what you are doing is wrong, you have won half the battle.*
- *Your parents may turn a blind eye, but you are the one who will lose the vision.*

Media: Making $$$ From Your Bad Choices

Andrew was in sixth grade and an exceptionally bright student with a very promising outlook on life. His older brother, Calvin, listened to hip-hop music as often as he could and played it loud enough so that Andrew could not help hearing the catchy rhythm and lyrics. He was intrigued by the sexually explicit nature of the lyrics, and the provocative photos of half-naked girls on the album covers really caught his attention. He would often sneak into his brother's room and look for more signs of risqué material.

He learned that it was perfectly common for women to be treated as mindless sex objects and that it was normal to demonstrate disrespectful behavior and abuse toward them. After all, almost every song he heard and picture he saw depicted that very message.

The more offensive, the more invigorating it became, and it made him feel hip and special too. Never once did it occur to him that something was amiss; he was young and unable to re-think his perception in terms of respecting a woman, or himself for that matter. He also figured that if his older brother was into it, then he must not be doing anything wrong.

All he knew was that it was very trendy to talk about sex and use really bad words at every opportunity. There were now images of half-naked women almost everywhere he looked. In fact, he soon started making a special effort to sneak a peek at the newsstand, video store, and he even knew where to find the adult magazines at his uncle's house. Pretty soon Andrew believed that everything worthwhile in life somehow revolved around sex.

He was young and immature, so how could he know that there was a whole different way? He was exposed to it everywhere and all the time. His parents were busy people and so never gave a second thought to the overflow of lewd material from Calvin's room. They were never really exposed to this type of world when they grew up, so they just brushed it off as nonsense, assuming that it would soon fade away. Besides, Andrew was too young and innocent and didn't really understand what he was hearing or seeing and by the time he was older, he would be into something else.

Andrew became obsessed with sex and nonchalant about bringing it up that one day he touched a girl inappropriately at school. He was immediately expelled as this was against the rules, and his gesture fell under the zero-tolerance policy adopted by so many schools today, especially those that really cared about their reputation and the quality of the education that their students received. His naive parents, who were of course oblivious and therefore very surprised, found it almost impossible to find a comparable school, one that would accept Andrew despite what he had done. Although extremely disappointed, they were basically responsible for Andrew falling into this trap.

Consequently, he now goes to a school where more than a few kids a grade higher are regularly acting inappropriately right on the school grounds: making out, smoking in the bathrooms, and pretty much doing anything and everything but preparing well for their futures.

Andrew's life had literally been turned upside down, and who knows if he will ever really recover from this act of foolishness. How will he adjust in accepting the new gateway to his future? Just as important and overlooked is the bigger question: Will he truly be able to love and respect a woman one day? Will he be able to successfully raise a warm, secure, and nurturing family? Will he sustain a monogamous relationship with his wife? With his attitude, environment, and circumstances, the chances look slim at best, so one can only hope.

Some of the media today is nothing short of pure evil. There are scores of despicable adults, most who have children of their own, that will feed any immoral filth into the young minds of children today just so they can make money. They make millions and millions of dollars mass-producing anything that lures kids to the dark side, while shielding their own children from watching or listening to what they put out there. As long as they can hide behind the notion that parents are to blame for letting their kids get exposed, they feel morally justified and simply pump up the volume.

It is clearly impossible, unless you lock children in a basement without windows for twenty-four hours a day, to hide them from the overwhelming decadence found around every corner. The mind bending smut is fine if it pollutes the minds of *other* people's children, sometimes incredibly even if it's their own children. Not that it is any consolation, but they too are naive as it is more often than not their own children that become affected by the industry in the worst possible way. There are alarming consequences for so many kids born into the entertainment world. The media as a whole have killed many a moral fiber that was and is needed to allow children to grow up into decent, caring, and respectable young adults who will then be called upon to raise a well-balanced families of their own one day.

It is very hard to fight because our country either has a tough time enforcing or entirely lacks laws that might prevent others from saying or doing practically anything in front of minors. Parents are quite helpless as they watch their beloved children grow up to disrespect authority and, worst of all, themselves. Scores of depraved individuals generally take what was once sacred and toss it aside to feed some of the depraved fantasies that are so openly pushed down the throats of young kids today.

It weakens the foundation of the nation that we belong to and tarnishes what we stand for as respectable citizens. There is absolutely no benefit to anyone (other than those who stand to benefit financially) to have children lose their innocence so young and to forego the values of respect and dignity. Some hide behind religion, which can and should be a good compass for morality, but even that is often filled with hypocrisy, corruption, and deceit in many cases.

Sex, alcohol, cigarettes, and decadence are also drugs, pushed so hard onto us by the media that they are often made to look like the catalyst to success and happiness. It frequently consumes at least a chapter or two of everyone's life, and then when it turns dangerous, everyone is surprised as the horror or ugliness shows up in their neighborhood. When one human under the influence of something intoxicating fails to respect another, or when one of them occasionally carries out unthinkable savagery on another, everyone is surprised and outraged. What did they expect?

Rape, murder, suicide, and torture are repeatedly glamorized by the media. Whether in a TV series, movie, a song, or the prime-time evening news, the media is counting on and feeding our thirst for violence, tragedy, and catastrophe, which is the ultimate *weapon of mass destruction*.

Our defenseless dedication to nourishing this media frenzy is all too common and clearly displays visible signs that the world is going mad. What are we to do?

Street Smart Tips

- *If you can't say it or do it in front of your own grandmother, then it is probably not cool.*
- *If you lose your self-respect, you will lose everyone's respect.*
- *Love songs have been replaced by sex songs.*

Adult Content And Immaturity

Andy found an adult magazine lying on the sidewalk one day. It was a very graphic magazine showing people doing things that one would not normally associate with normal behavior. Andy was a young 10, young enough for him to not fully understand everything he saw. So, from that day on, Andy perceived this to be the typical behavior that would be expected of him when he was a little older.

There were several men and women in all different positions, and they were doing things and dressed in ways that he just could not grasp. There were images of women being restrained and possibly being hurt. It was all so confusing and captivating, but none of it made any sense. It did feel weird, so he just did not say anything to anyone.

For many years Andy kept this dark secret to himself, but he could never get the images out of his mind. He could not ask anyone because somehow he just could not bring himself to discuss this with anyone he knew. He just figured that when he was older, those weird but interesting images would be normalized. He accepted it as a part of his understanding of what sex would be all about and why people had to wait until they were older—perhaps because sex was scary.

A few years later, Andy was old enough to have a girlfriend and after a few months of being together, he finally made reference to the images and activities that were still haunting him after all these years. Surprising to Andy, this lovely girl he became so very fond of now thought of him as creepy and abnormal and unexpectedly wanted nothing more to do with him.

Eventually, after losing more than a few relationships this way, Andy soon came to realize that most people he encountered were either unaware or completely disinterested in this type of behavior.

But instead of just forgetting about it, and to satisfy his lingering curiosity, he started searching for the type of people who were into this sort of thing. When he finally came into contact with a few of these over-the-top individuals, he soon realized that they were missing a whole lot of what he considered sacred and normal in life.

In spite of this, the challenge that he now had to face was going to be whether or not he could manage his own perception of what being in a loving relationship was and whether or not he was always going to be at risk of losing a good relationship by pushing it a little too far over that edge. When things seemed a little less exciting, as they often might in any somewhat stable and everyday relationship, it became very hard for him to deal with it.

Due to the complacency of many parents, children, who are by no means mature enough, are allowed to see R-rated movies or listen to X-rated music. Though they are exposed to content they are not old enough or mature enough to fully understand, they are seldom deemed old enough to take on responsibilities around house, read the newspaper, get a summer job, feed the pets, wash the car, or do any of the many unpleasant chores that are reserved for adults.

Why would parents give in to all the fun things that kids want to do that result in growing up way too fast, while they do not always take the time to teach them useful and necessary life skills to understand exactly what they are exposed to outside of the home? Many parents also try very hard to protect their children from stressful lives; they send them to good schools, teach them to be careful and avoid danger, but then allow them to run wild and be in contact with some seriously mind-altering "artistic" garbage. Some things really are for adults only. Not for any other reason than an adult mind has matured and can distinguish certain rights from wrongs. There is no substitute for maturity. Adults may be less influenced than the younger generation.

How many parents really know where their teenagers are at all times, what drugs they take, how much alcohol they drink, how fast they drive, and how many other kids they have sex with on a regular basis? Many parents prefer not to know just so they don't have to deal with it. We call this being "in denial." Still, this does not eliminate the problem. Some parents are okay gambling with the lives of their own flesh and blood. It is easier than getting involved because it's too hard to keep up with it all, they are too busy, or they believe that their kids would never indulge. As long as their kids don't get arrested or killed, everything is fine and dandy. Of course if and when they do, it's obviously and tragically too late for tears.

Believe it or not, many kids do crave more parental involvement over their freedoms, but they seldom admit it because relationships with a parent are often just too difficult to manage. It's more common than you might think.

Given all the challenges, what sensible preventive measures can be taken by parents in our society? Many of today's parents are either simply naive, are too preoccupied, or too selfish to put in the time and effort needed to teach their kids to be safe, learn street smarts, and be wise enough to survive the many missiles of temptation. Is it someone else's responsibility to teach their kids about the dangers of knowing too much too soon? By doing grown-up activities before they are actually mature enough to understand them, children are sometimes irrevocably damaged.

Will one parent's lack of proper parenting one day cost his or her children's friends their lives? Occasionally, it is a parent's lack of good judgment in teaching their own kids well that leads to the demise of someone else's kids. For instance, the irresponsible practice of drunk driving resulting in the death of another's son or daughter is not such a random occurrence; it happens time and time again.

Yes, we can blame the parents, but remember blame occurs after the tragedy has already happened, when it arguably doesn't really matter anymore. While exercising street smarts or using common sense, it is possible to prevent so many of the tragedies from happening at all. While this may all sound very much like adult-orientated ranting, the things that young people don't really want to hear, you have already been exposed to a lot of the bad, but it's not too late for all *smart* kids to stand up for themselves and accept the truth, regardless of what was or was not taught in the home.

Street Smart Tips

- *If your parents forget to teach you something important, you will have to learn it somewhere else, most likely the hard way or from the wrong person.*
- *Once you know something, you own it, so be very careful of what you don't want to learn!*
- *The thing about immaturity is that immature kids are usually too immature to realize that they are immature. (a critical roadblock to overcome)*

Chapter Nine

Parents & Kids—Roles And Responsibilities

Mary and Mike are very much in love and are the proud but anxious parents of a cute little baby boy. Mary is, however, still in college and did not expect to fall pregnant, but she and Mike, high-school sweethearts promised one another to be together forever, no matter what. It was of course quite a chore taking care of little Tommy, and Mary consequently could not study as much as she felt was needed to pass her courses. Mike could not take any time off work and, other than earning a wage, was unable to help much with raising Tommy.

In fact there were days that he had to work overtime, which was fortunate because they really needed the money, but when he walked into the apartment at eight o'clock, he would sometimes find Mary dozing on the couch, exhausted, while little Tommy crawled aimlessly around the apartment. He would often find little Tommy hungry and dirty, and this made him feel very frustrated and guilty at the same time. He understood that Mary was under way too much pressure and that she really wanted to go to college to improve her chances for the future, but he could not help getting furious at her for not keeping Tommy in a suitable environment for a growing toddler.

They started to fight regularly, and soon Mary had to give up on her dreams of becoming a nurse and drop out of school to find a job. Tommy was put in a day care center and this made both Mike and Mary very unhappy; Mike was constantly despondent, and the constant strain eventually took a severe toll on their relationship. Tommy was now growing up in a very negative environment, surrounded by strangers all day long, and then the constant yelling at night ensured that he was quite confused at his tender age of just eighteen months. This constant source of stress and inability to work things out led to the eventual separation of Mike and Mary and, ultimately, to little Tommy's being sent to live with Mary's parents as a last resort. Mike seldom saw him because "it was just too hard" for one reason or another.

Tommy became another product of a broken home. Mike and Mary now hated one another and Mary's parents could not keep up with the demands of raising a young child and had to eventually seek a foster home for Tommy. Everyone's intentions were good from the beginning but, unfortunately, at everyone's expense, most especially little Tommy's, they all had to give up. There was just no way, even with the best intentions that a young family could manage through these circumstances. Sure, they were all victims, but what chance was Tommy going to have at living a normal, safe, and nurturing life given the way things had already started?

Parents take on an immensely HUGE responsibility when they decide to bring a child into the world, intentionally or not. Many, if not most, do not know what they are signing up for. By bringing a new baby into the world, they theoretically and morally promise to give this helpless, extremely dependant infant creature the mere basics consisting of food and water, shelter from the elements, safety from harm, education to function, attention, emotional security, and a funny little thing called love.

We have all heard about these basic necessities before, but let's take a closer look at what each of these promises might actually entail.

Clean water and food that is nutritious and promotes well-being is a good start. Scientific evidence shows that kids need a well-balanced diet consisting of all the vitamins, grains, and minerals to give their immune systems a fighting chance as they enter a very complex, sometimes polluted, and ever-changing, unpredictable environment.

Shelter is not necessarily a mansion, but it should at least be somewhere clean and comfortable. It should protect a child from the harsh climate, predators, disease, and any possible external danger. This shelter should ideally encompass a sanitary and healthy setting devoid of harmful elements such as cigarette smoke, unsafe chemicals, inconsistent temperatures, incessant noise, and any other avoidable, unpleasant surroundings.

Safety can be a habitat in which a child is protected from physical and emotional harm. Some unsuspecting or naive parents often leave their children in the care of incompetent, irresponsible, or unstable people, only to find out years later that their loved ones were abused and were subjected to life-altering horrors that never go away.

Early education, according to our logical social standards, includes learning skills necessary for survival. There are the basics such as personal hygiene, the understanding of bathroom and kitchen dangers, or any other possible hazardous area or appliance, in and around the house. Later on, parents focus on protecting their children from less apparent but equally harmful influences such as today's social, psychological, and virtual hazards.

Love and affection! Well, this one is wide open. What might any parent be expected to do or sacrifice so that his or her offspring can have more than a fighting chance in life? Money helps (and often hurts), but it is far from the main ingredient required to put this very important verb in force. How much time, energy, and effort will parents put into their children's well-being? All kids, rich or poor, are at risk of life becoming way too much for the parents to adequately handle. It is just as often the "well to do" parents who come up short when giving their children the tools to have a balanced and stable life. The correct amount of attention for any particular child is critical in the pursuit of a practical and manageable life.

On the other hand, the lack of a good mix of constructive attention often leads to a life of confusion, insecurity, and frustration, which is then passed on from one generation to another.

Having street smarts can sometimes be described as the ability to take enough of what does work over what is proven not to work and apply it proportionately to fit into your personality, lifestyle, and particular ambitions.

Street Smart Tips

- *No one can protect you from yourself; that's your responsibility.*
- *Listen to your parents and your teachers carefully and be sure you actually understand what they mean.*
- *Never be afraid to ask anyone about anything, it's almost always OK.*

Breaking News

It is important to realize that parents are people too, and people are not perfect—not my parents, not your parents, not anyone's parents. However tough as it is to accept, some parents are just totally inept and therefore do more harm than good to their kids. Blatantly speaking, far too many parents should never have had kids, but they did, and maybe, just maybe, that kid is you or me.

But, like you, parents need to be understood, tolerated, and supported. Most do their very best even though their very best may just not be good enough in some circumstances.

Accept this and move on, just as soon as you can, mentally that is. Crazy as it may seem, one day you will help them for they cannot help themselves. Nowhere does it say that your parents are automatically smarter or better informed than you. Sure, they know more about many things in the beginning because they have been around longer, but they may have limitations when trying to help you take on the big wide world in any meaningful way. When they get stuck, and one day they will, you are basically left to your own devices to make important decisions. And later on, blaming others when things don't work out will not change the outcome but it will serve as another reminder of how important it is to take care of some things *yourself*.

Now more than ever, not only do you have to face the world and all its detours on your own, but in order to create a life of balance, you will first have to figure out just how badly you are off track, fix it, and get back in the game, ready to win. It's sad to say, but parents (and then society) are the principal cause of the large numbers of disadvantaged kids. Most parents will deny it because *they don't know* that *they didn't know* how to make things better for you. But if *you* rise to the occasion and still give parents a fighting chance, you can help them to make it much better for both of you. This is a tough challenge, but how you see, treat, and interact with your own parents and other adults can make a significant difference in how they respect you and, ultimately, how your own life turns out.

First thing is to be super open-minded and to set aside the destructive emotions, stubbornness, and feelings of inequity that may be clouding your vision and judgment.

This is the biggest thing you have to do. *Take a look at your situation objectively,* as if you were a bird flying up above and looking down, observing your actual life, *your actions and specifically your reactions.*

You can now easily see what is working for you and what is not. It's no longer an opinion or an emotion, it's now an observed fact and facts are true, and truth is reality, whether you like it or not!

Doing this will make you a lot *more aware* in several important areas, things will be much clearer, easier to appreciate and better understood.

Now, get ready to take the second step and start making your life a little better, one day at a time!

Is A Parent's Love Unconditional?

Think about it. Would you help clean up your friend's soiled pants if he or she had a stinky accident right next to you, right now? You would probably run a mile; *it's so disgusting, phew, aaagh, no!*

So, can you now imagine that your parent(s), OK maybe not always both of them, without a second thought, would clean up your stinky butt, your runny nose, or your throw up, no matter how nasty you made it for them or where they were at the time that you needed service. This may be a little too graphic, but it is one notable example of how unconditional love works. And the visual I've provided might make you remember it well. Consider too that the overwhelming majority of parents would do anything for their kids—anytime and anywhere. No matter how awkward, inconvenient, disgusting, dangerous, or embarrassing the situation, parents are usually the only ones who come through for you every time. No questions asked.

A cold, hard fact is that there are and will be very few people in the world with whom you will be that connected throughout your life. Most relationships come and go, yes even the really good ones when you are growing up. People change all the time. Many move away and very few will step up when you are in dire need. In fact, as unfortunate as it may seem, you might never find anyone for the rest of your life who will take care of you in such an unconditional way, and the older you get, the more likely it is that you will be tackling life solo.

Way down the road when you really need someone to care about you in less of a romantic and in more of a critical way, you'll want to have someone in your life. There is no substitute for the way in which little old married couples love and care for each other in sickness and in health, especially after spending decades together.

Now more than ever, people generally live longer and in their old age are more likely to need someone to help them bathe, eat, take meds, visit the bathroom, and even get dressed.

I can think of only one thing as sad as a lonely child; it is a lonely old person, especially when the ability to take care of himself or herself has diminished considerably. Many old people die without an ounce of dignity and in front of complete strangers, and it will only become more common the longer we live. The circle of life could be well enough defined as parents taking care of children and then children taking care of parents, and so on. Sometimes both unavoidable and avoidable circumstances break the cycle, and basic living conditions become quite disheartening.

Receiving real love is such an extraordinary and precious experience, and yet so many people grow up without it. Some, on the other hand, are fortunate enough to have lots of love available but fail to appreciate it or choose to disregard it, thus breaking the hearts and spirits of many (who are simply other vulnerable creatures) without a second thought because they have selfishly taken the giver's devotion for granted. There are parents crying all over the world because their kids, whom they love more than life itself, have chosen to reject them over some seemingly minor misunderstanding or disagreement. Many relationships are broken and remain so because of selfish pride, jealousy, stubbornness, greed, laziness, apathy, or simply because someone's feelings were once hurt in the heat of the moment.

Of course there are many good reasons why family members and friends no longer get along, but *it is worth fixing if possible*. If just a third of all the bad parent–children relationships in the world were reinstated, an undeniable positive impact on the quality of our society would result. I will explain more as you continue reading.

If you have the power to *reinstate or protect a loving relationship*, seriously consider making the required effort to do so.

Street Smart Tips

- *Often, the person you are waiting for is actually waiting for you. Be sure to check.*
- *Being proud and having pride is not the same thing.*
- *Love is a verb, not a noun.*

What Is Responsibility?

Bobby was nine years old and, at his school, was considered to be a well-adjusted kid with good friends and decent grades. Not too many people knew though that Bobby was really a super lazy kid and did nothing to help his mom around the house. In fact, just like his father, he rarely picked up his clothing from the floor or washed a dish that he ate from. Both his parents worked very hard, and when his mom came home from work he often yelled at her for not feeding him quickly enough or because his favorite shirt was not laundered.

His mom had a very soft heart and, although exhausted from a hard day at work, would drop everything to take care of Bobby's needs just so that he would not be so rude or disrespectful to her. When she went to bed at the end of a long day, she would cry herself to sleep. It was just too much and she could not cope, so she sobbed into her pillow so as not to disturb her sleeping husband.

Eventually, she saw a doctor who quickly prescribed a medication to help her to relieve some of her anxiety. One of the side effects of her prescription was to make her feel more relaxed, so, consequently, she got less done quickly. But her relationship with her son and husband became less filled with angst, at least for her because she did not really care that much anymore. She found that the little pills made her "cope," so she did not go a day without them. Pretty soon she needed more and more to keep the effect going, and soon she could not function without them. This caused all kinds of new problems at home, none of which made it easier to rescue her relationship with her family.

Being selfish for so long, they really had no easy way of coping with her in her state and either got mad, frustrated, or just ignored her most of the time. All she really needed in the beginning was a little consideration, a little help around the house, or a little break once in a while, but, instead, she lost what was once most dear to her: her family.

Being a kid is a one-shot deal. Once you lose it, it is gone forever. Theoretically, being a kid is the best part of your life. The rest is good, too, but being a little kid is very special and does not last nearly as long as being an adult. For many there are innocent laugh-out-loud good times, not-a-worry-in-the-world attitudes, pure love, no hate, no resentment, no racism, no judgment, no betrayal, no violence, no lies, no deceit, no anxiety, no stress, and on and on. Why we throw it all away as soon as we can is beyond all logic.

There are, unfortunately, many kids who do not have the luxury of being kids for very long. If you are one of the lucky ones living in a loving household, be sure to cherish it, but consider demonstrating some appreciation for this privilege.

Being a grown-up is forever. You might have as many as eighteen years of being a dependent kid versus a possible sixty to seventy years of not being one, so think about why you would want to rush through it as fast as you can, which leads to the next question: how about participating in the process of making growing up a good thing in your home? Help a little, be considerate, and contribute to the harmony so that everyone under the same roof is having fun. It is most often the realism that being at home is not that much fun anyway that drives kids to want early independence. But remember, being a kid is one shot, and there are no second chances!

While having the best of intentions, parents are often limited in their capabilities, resources, and support to understand what makes their kids independent and resourceful. It is a fine line with no easy guidelines. It can go either way—too much attention or not enough.

Parents, who work long hours or have two jobs, just to make ends meet, are often doing more harm than good. They want to provide a good life filled with goodies for their kids, but they never really see their children or spend any quality time with them; they become tired and unhealthy and generally miss out on the whole idea of raising a family. Actually, children can make a huge difference if they help run the house, when they can, by doing small but important chores. Kids who just sit around while their parents work all day and then watch them frantically trying to make dinner, wash the dishes, clean up the kitchen, do homework, take out the garbage, make lunches, and pay bills are what you might call spoiled rotten.

It does not have much to do with how wealthy the family is but more to do with how much appreciation each family member has for the other. Spoiled is bad, bad for today and bad for the future. Spoiled children often have more permanent problems in life than those who were not spoiled when they were growing up. It is likely that well-adjusted, unselfish, and less demanding children will do a much better job of managing their own future, including their relationships later on in life.

It is possible to help relieve some of the pressure that parents go through with the understanding that, right or wrong, your parents are trying to give you a better life, and that should not be taken for granted. However, they may be missing the whole point and chasing after short-term gratification while severely impairing the long-term benefits of a structured household. Single-parent families or dads of the "never home" type families are even more at risk, but most kids can help in small and effective ways.

You can do small things to help around the house, and even small gestures go a long way to make the family unit stronger. Every little thing that kids do for themselves frees the parents up a little and releases the stress some, allowing for a more calm and harmonious home atmosphere. The physical help is not to be ignored as everyone could use a hand, but the emotional and physiological health of a sharing and caring environment is immeasurably good, and the outcome of this type of family unit can be very positive in so many ways. It is not just about saying "thank you" every day but more about stepping up and taking on some of the day-to-day demands that require attention. It is about making a house a cherished and healthy home that will produce support, goodwill and a good old-fashioned loving family!

These small but critical loads that are taken off the backs of parents allow them to enjoy life a little, too. When parents are happier and stress-free, they can take the time and energy needed to be better parents, friends, and citizens. It is a win-win for all; just a little unselfish caring goes a long, long way.

Remember, parents are people too; people with needs, faults, and shortcomings but typically with good intentions that include making your life better- way better than you can make it without them. If they are trying, and you know that they really are, a little reciprocation will go a long way. (That definitely goes for teachers too)

Street Smart Tips

- *You will definitely experience a lot of what your parents go through one day, but you don't have to wait to understand.*
- *You will become just like your parents in some ways; pay good attention to this.*
- *Your parents were once kids too; they are not that naive.*

Chapter Ten

Friends And Influence

Sherry was a sweet, shy country girl who had dreams of a fairytale wedding one day. When she was just sixteen she met Chelsea, a provocative, sexy, and flirtatious big- city- girl who was obviously very intriguing to others. Boys wanted to get to know her, and girls wanted to be like her. She was confident and flamboyant, and that drew a lot of attention even on the rare occasion that she was not really trying. Sherry felt quite special to be the friend of someone so popular.

Then one day it became evident that Chelsea was popular for good reason, because she was having sex with many of the boys, and it was even rumored that with some girls, too. She told her very upset and confused friend, Sherry, that it was no big deal and that she should loosen up and not be so serious about life. Sherry was visibly uncomfortable with this notion and immediately started to feel a distance grow between them.

Chelsea was having the time of her life and certainly not giving Sherry's discomfort too much thought, leaving Sherry to become withdrawn and feeling somewhat lonely and disappointed.

After a while (pretty soon actually), Sherry decided that in order to remain popular with Chelsea and the others, she had to be more like her and so she changed her behavior to become a little easier with the boys, too. Unfortunately, and unpredictably, she contracted a sexually transmitted disease, one that would never go away and this made her very angry and bitter. She was so furious that she now slept around even more and soon earned the reputation of being super easy, shredding her country-girl image to bits. This went on for years; she slept with almost every guy in her grade until she finally grew out of it and went to off to college. Sherry studied hard and eventually became a top designer in New York. She made great money, had a promising career, and then, as is quite common, she wanted a husband and a family to feel complete.

One day, by chance, Sherry ran into an old school friend, Tom Collins, who was one year older, in the lobby of a prestigious high-rise building on Fifth Avenue. He was a prominent good-looking lawyer who worked a few floors above her, and she soon learned that he was what one would refer to as a highly eligible bachelor.

He was very friendly, even a little flirtatious, but he never did ask her out despite their bumping into each other a half a dozen or so times at the coffee shop downstairs. So, she decided to take the initiative and ask him to join her for dinner or drinks one night. He politely refused, saying that although he did find her quite attractive, he just could not allow their relationship to develop. She was visibly disappointed and a little embarrassed and did not pursue it further.

One day a few months later, and after being driven crazy over this rejection, she plucked up the courage to call him and ask him why he was so disinterested in furthering their relationship. To this he bluntly replied that although he found it very difficult to resist her and that he too was ready for a serious relationship, he just couldn't ever contemplate being married to her and having a family after what he knew about her past. He further explained that if he ever bumped into anyone from their school, and added he knew that they would one day, it would be forever acknowledged that he was married to the girl with the worst reputation for sleeping around at Tremor High. He added that he was sorry but that he just did not have the stomach to deal with that for the rest of his life, nor did he ever want his children to have to deal with something like that when they got older. After that, they never saw or spoke to each other again.

Your friends will make or break you. Really good friends won't even know that they are empowering you to do better, and their positive influence perpetuated by their actions and attitude will take you further than you can imagine. The better they do, the better you do. It's a natural progression to want to keep up. Congenial envy and friendly competition is a very good thing. Parents will almost always want their child to be in a competitive environment so that the positive influence of others will rub off on them. It is very healthy to want to improve, and it can be even better when you have achieved a level worthy enough to help others to succeed.

On the other hand, bad friends will consciously encourage you to engage in mischievous or shameful behavior because the worse that you do, the better it will make them look and feel about themselves. They get to think more of themselves by comparison when you do awful things. The more you fail and the deeper the trouble you find yourself in, the better they appear by comparison.

It is sad to say that even the best of friends sometimes bet against each other, secretly hoping for the other to fail. It makes you think, doesn't it?

Is it a "friend" who first introduces you to drugs, alcohol, or promiscuity, or might they be considered the worst kind of enemy, a wolf in sheep's clothing? Be smart about this very important and difficult to swallow realization; you will only ever make very few *true* friends in your life. The real definition of a friend will not be found in a dictionary as someone that will encourage you to get drunk, do drugs, or do dangerous things with them because it's just going to be more fun, and they can't do it if you don't. A friend will also not be defined in any way as someone who will help you to potentially destroy your life.

Once you recognize a *true* friend, someone who actually persuades you to say no, because they plan to be in your life a long time, you absolutely must do all you can to be the true friend back to them. If not, this apparent friendship that was made in heaven will soon dissipate along with the hundreds of other short-lived relationships that you get to experience throughout the rest of your life.

As mentioned before, of the literally thousands of people you will meet in your lifetime, less than a handful of them will be there for you when you really need them in the future. On the other hand, bad friends are everywhere; they come and go spreading their ill will, taking what they can, doing or saying anything to make their lives better, albeit at your expense. Once it is obvious they can't use you anymore, they will move on to another sucker, leaving you disappointed, disillusioned, less trusting, and now less capable of making really good friends in the future.

We do typically remember the hurt and hold onto the bad memory from the past, so beware of losing the ability to trust in the future because of the bad judgment you made when you chose your last group of friends.

Be *smart* and choose your friends wisely because every time you lose a "good friend," you typically lose a little of what it takes to be a good friend to someone else.

Street Smart Tips

- *Be cautious and within reason; give to a friendship without expecting to receive.*
- *Even your very best friend is capable of breaking your heart.*
- *It does not have to be intentional or premeditated, but some friendships are often doomed to die before they start.*

Impressing "Good" Friends

It is both normal and expected to want to impress the people that you call your friends. After all, if you are not somewhat impressive you might not have any friends at all. Be very aware, though, of the superficial behavior that one often mistakes for genuine care. It takes a while to know if someone is genuinely interested in you or more concerned about who you are or what you have. Be open-minded, but don't let your guard down too soon.

It is also very easy to impress a fool with foolish behavior. Think carefully about what kind of person will want to be your friend if they are impressed by crude material or meaningless acts of irrational behavior. If you only impress someone by acting irresponsibly or foolishly, what might that say about them?

Alternatively, if you look around and all of your friends are acting like idiots, then it's time to ask yourself, "What am I really getting from these relationships?" It's not that you need to always take something from every relationship, but at some point there should be a little mutual respect, admiration, and stimulation for you to want to spend all your valuable time in their company. If your friends bring your level of behavior down, it's probably time to think about upgrading.

Be aware that although showing good character should be long lasting, these so-called friends will let you hang out with them so long as they are impressed by you and your stuff, but they will be long gone when they find other friends with better stuff or more to offer them. If you want to impress someone, the right someone, try to impress them with your standards, ethics, and level of commitment to something truly worthwhile. These are the things that last forever, and a true friend will cherish that. The so-called stuff is never good enough for very long, and you are better off without those types taking up your headspace.

Peer Pressure

Peer pressure too can be either good or bad, but in this chapter the focus is on why you would want to be like someone else. The best case scenario is that you are considered a copycat and don't really have your own identity.

Remember, any situation—especially one including drugs and alcohol—affects people differently. If your friend can handle six drinks and walk straight afterward, but you get queasy from just one, you must have the common sense to realize that what does not affect one person very much may well make another sick, or perhaps really mess them up in some way. After a wildly insane party, your friend goes home and wakes up with a headache the next morning, and you, on the other hand, started something that turns into a world of hurt.

As soon as you become needy, that very same friend that got you started on the path to destruction will be long gone. Does it really ever make good sense?

Are you considered cool if you follow your friends down Demolition Avenue, or are you cooler if you say, "No, there's a better road I know"? You may not realize it at the time because you don't want to be ridiculed, mocked, or not accepted, but you will eventually learn that being really cool is about being able to say no and more so when you are confident enough to tell someone else to say no, too. This is the sign of a true leader and a real winner who may save a life rather than be responsible for wasting one, maybe even your own. You may be too young or naive to know it right now, but take this information with you; it may really come in handy one day. Following is easy; in fact, we all follow someone and few rarely lead, but the most admired people in the world are typically leaders in some capacity; and the others, well, if they are smart enough to follow the right leaders, they too will be just fine.

Your parents, your teachers, your bosses, your music and movie idols, and eventually your very own kids can leave you dumbstruck with their ability to lead you in some aspect of your life.

Consider following a path that allows you to learn about leadership and through this you will instinctively learn responsibility and accountability.

It is a fact that most responsible people get to enjoy more of life's wonderful little gifts along the way.

Street Smart Tips

- *You will rarely still be friends in the future with those that seem most important to you today; spend your energy wisely.*
- *There is love and then there is hate, both require the same amount of effort.*
- *Your friends will have other friends, as will you; manage your expectations accordingly.*

Reputation

This is huge! Your reputation is one of the most precious intangible assets that you will ever own. It takes years to earn it and just seconds to lose it, and you cannot believe how today's modern technology has changed the game.

Almost anything that you do to hurt your reputation can and will most likely stay with you forever. Try as you might, you will never escape it and, one day, when you least expect it or need it, your past antics might ruin the opportunity of a lifetime. It can cost you dearly, possibly altering your destiny.

In earlier years, you could typically get away with a sordid past, small conviction, or questionable accusation, but today, you might find yourself defending yourself by trying to explain something that happened up to thirty years ago, and I challenge you to argue that it will be a pleasant experience or considered not to be a "big deal".

Your reputation will either open or close doors for you throughout your entire life, doors you may really want to pass through. Think twice before using the old "young and foolish" defense. There is a hard drive out there just waiting to jog someone's memory.

Street Smart Tips

- *What might be good for one person could well be poison for another.*
- *The friends that influence you in a bad way will almost never be your friends for very long, so it is better not to invest the time in the first place.*
- *If you have had to be pressured even slightly into doing anything, step back for a second and think twice about it.*

Sincerity

This is the silent assassin of a reputation. Simply put, if you are an insincere person, you will have no *real* friends. Since people will believe they can't rely on you or trust you, they will spend their energy trying to get closer to other people. You will most often be unaware of it, but they will likely badmouth you to everyone that will listen, making it even tougher for you to make new friends. People will then shy away from you to avoid disappointment and to prevent wasting their precious time with you because they have heard that you can't be expected to keep your word.

Believe it or not, people do like to gossip and will sometimes even exaggerate a story for more impact. Try not to be the subject of someone else's gossip story, unless it's a really good one and in your favor. Once you get known for being insincere or unreliable, you will inherently lose out on some valuable opportunities. You will not be near the top on too many lists and no one will want to help you to be successful or make your life easier.

Consequently, many people known to be insincere subsequently *get let down themselves* at the worst possible times, like when they really need help in a tough situation.

Almost all people who enjoy some success in their lives were given a break along the way from someone in a position to help them, to help themselves. These are the generous folks who have made it in life and who will almost always choose someone that has proven to be trustworthy, reliable, and sincere and, therefore, the most deserving of the opportunity they are providing.

We are talking about life-altering opportunities that often create substantial wealth, security, and ultimately a life filled with really good quality experiences.

Trustworthiness is an earned treasure that, once lost, cannot ever be bought back, no matter how rich you are. Even though you will be naturally *smarter* the next time around, you will nevertheless have to start from the very bottom.

Street Smart Tips

- *It takes a long time to develop trust in someone but only a moment for him or her to destroy it for good.*
- *Your reputation follows you everywhere you go, forever.*
- *Technology has made sure that all your mistakes are permanently recorded for anyone to see at any time.*

Chapter Eleven

Comfort Zone

James is a somewhat insecure kid. He sits on a bench alone everyday watching the other kids interact in the schoolyard, laughing out loud and making plans for the weekend, as if they do not have a care in the world. He yearns to be included, and he constantly wonders how to become one of the gang.

Frustrated and somewhat desperate, he begins dressing noticeably differently from the others in the attempt to get some attention. According to most adults, his hair looks ridiculous; his color coordination is off the mark; and it is not too long before he overhears a few kids snicker about how his bizarre appearance makes him look like a freak. He becomes more and more agitated with everyone and is eventually forced to hang around with anyone that will tolerate him, specifically a group of kids on the fast track to nowhere who think it's kind of cool to be odd and different where, basically, anything goes.

He soon starts smoking and drinking anything offered to him and vandalizing property as a dare, just to fit in and win over his new "friends." What he doesn't realize, though, is that they couldn't care less about him anyway, they simply see him as entertainment. They treat him well enough by his standards, and so he finally feels important. He feels like he belongs, and that is a good thing for James.

It is not too long before James gets arrested with two of the other kids and is detained in a juvenile hall for almost two weeks because, unlike the others, his parents could not get it together to pay any bail. He is forced to live with some pretty scary, messed up kids and while incarcerated learns about the circumstances that led some of them to this unfortunate place. He suddenly comes to realize that he is heading down the wrong road and gets enough of a fright to recognize that his recent choices were not good ones. With time on his hands, James thinks a lot about his future.

Since he does have a mild interest in cooking, when he gets out he borrows money from an aunt and enrolls himself into an evening cooking class. On the second night, he meets Jean who becomes a friend to him and introduces him to her roommate, Sybil. Sybil and James also share a common interest in watching classic movies and, pretty soon, they start going to the local theater together. There they meet up with another couple from Sybil's high school and soon become friends. They eventually find themselves meeting up with other movie enthusiasts as well. Before you know it, they belong to an informal little club that meets every Friday night to see the movie of the week. Within a couple of months, they are twelve strong, and life among this group of friends is better and far more stimulating than James could ever have imagined.

James was clearly the unofficial leader of the group, which made him feel very accomplished. It took a little jolt, which, fortunately, did not end too disastrously, to make him realize that there was plenty of room for him in the world; he just had to look in the right places and exercise a little common sense and patience.

We all have a comfort zone in which we feel important. This zone is determined by how we view ourselves in the world and with whom we want to hang out on a regular basis. It is largely influenced by our social standing, education, *self-esteem*, and our physical and emotional appearance to others. As humans, we all need a group to belong to; it can be a small group or a large group, and we can choose to be the leader of that group or participate as an appreciated and respected member. Either one is fine so long as you are comfortable with your role in the group, and the other members are accepting of your position.

Groups come in various forms and vary greatly with many different themes that hinge on anything from religion, sports, academics, nationality, and charitable organizations to crime, extreme cruelty, gangs, or jail buddies. You are still free to choose the group to which you want to belong and are unrestricted in giving it your best shot as a contributing member. Of course, the group you choose could have a positive or negative influence on you and others. It could be quite difficult to join but, even worse, the wrong group can be difficult, if not impossible, to leave.

The dangers of belonging to the wrong group—one that does not value justice, fairness, honesty, or integrity—could of course have detrimental effects on your life. The groups that have minimal qualifications for entry, or just want your money, are certainly not going to be the most prestigious groups. They will typically prey on vulnerable individuals who usually have low self-esteem, low self-respect, and who are in need of anyone that will accept them.

These groups are easy for anyone to join, but you will eventually realize that they do not offer anything of value in return. After all, if you are not in a very good state of mind, they will promise you the world, and you might just fall for it. They are also typically good at persuading you to try very difficult, if not impossible, tasks that they are trained to make look easy. You will often meet the kind of people that you really shouldn't, convincing people who will bring you nothing but bad luck and waste your time, all while helping you to spend your last dollar. The further away you get from these people, the better.

It is not uncommon to belong to this kind of group until you realize they are simply deceitful and have all kinds of prepared excuses for when they are "found out." It could be that you are hooked on the hype they provide or the excitement you feel when they are selling to you. Or, you are so committed to the "opportunity" that you lose everything if you walk away, which, by the way, typically happens anyway; but you wait it out until you just lose more. The consequences of joining the wrong group are usually very costly and can take years to fix.

By default, you do already belong to certain groups, respectable or not. You may choose not to participate to a great degree, but any way you look at it, you always have a place where you do belong. You might also want to re-think some of the warm and genuine invitations extended to you in the past, those opportunities that you blew off at the time as unexciting, too time consuming, or too educational, but which you now know are actually quite beneficial, as long as *they* do not have any good reason to exclude you. Of course, there will always be those groups that you will want to get away from as quickly as possible, and then there are those that you cannot ever escape from, so, at best, you will need to keep a very low profile.

In the big scheme of things, we already know that everything we learn is taught by someone else who had the knowledge before us. If you don't read about it somewhere, you might get to learn about it from a teacher, or it could be from a TV personality, a radio announcer, a coach, or a salesman, but a friend, peer, or a fellow group member is easily your best teacher. Typically, they are the people we know and trust; it is from them that we are getting the best knowledge and information.

So, the biggest benefit to being part of a good group with a worthy cause is the sound and dependable knowledge and advice they will share with you. On top of that, and perhaps as important, is the opportunity to make a new good friend or two along the way. Good friends can literally save your life, meaning they bring value, interest, and excitement to an otherwise uneventful or disappointing existence.

Real friendship is arguably the most valuable treasure in life. It is unconditional friendship that people seek most often. True friendships are developed over time, nurtured, and earned and should, therefore, be taken care of with extreme thoughtfulness and consideration. A good friendship can make a life worth living, but I must mention that a friendship that ends badly can really hurt.

Life is all about balance, and so being aware of equal but powerful contrary emotions is critical. It is believed to be well worth the risk of losing a friend just to have had one or to have experienced being in love, despite things not lasting forever. In fact, anything worth taking the time and patience to create can be, and usually is, very difficult to lose.

Functional groups can be considered a collection of like-minded people with common goals. Finding the right group to belong to will typically change the status of your life, bringing meaning, compassion, and self-worth. Finding a group can of course be a challenge, but a challenge that could easily be overcome by starting a group of your own. Select individuals with a common mind-set, and then see just how far forward your new group can go while bringing synchronized harmony to your own world. There is certainly no need to live life alone; it usually does not yield the best results.

It has been said that happiness is seldom described well, but you will certainly know it when you feel it.

Street Smart Tips

- *People with different talents and ideas but with similar interests make for a good group.*
- *A group setting is helpful in many areas of one's life, especially when it comes to motivation and support.*
- *There are many important ambitions in life that simply cannot be achieved without the involvement of a diverse group of people.*

Distractions And Influences

Although you can benefit greatly from being surrounded by other people, it is important to realize that they can be and often are the source of many distractions. These distractions come in all forms (it's not just the promise of money); and they, too, are basically good and perhaps not so good. Either way, they greatly affect each one of us throughout our lives, sometimes requiring tremendous resources.

There are movements, media influences, rumors, shiny objects, and promises of success that persuade many people. And often without them realizing it, they get sucked deep into bad situations. Then there are the many popular icons that live a seemingly untouchable and thrilling life, and this ideology can influence the behavior of millions of ordinary people who will change their values and ideals to their own detriment. The emulation of another or the pursuit of their enviable lifestyle most often ends in severe disillusionment.

When reality takes precedence over the initial infatuation, hopes and dreams are quickly crushed, leaving a void where your own unique soul once lived.

Many of us are very easily distracted, usually because real hard work is often disguised as an easy way out or a fast track to riches, and so we live our entire lives chasing the assurance of victory that is so frivolously offered to us by one or more unscrupulous people. This can lead to a life of insignificance and despondency, often ending in regret and depression.

Some distractions can be very constructive, and there is plenty of good to learn if you are prepared to raise your basic level of attentiveness and, most importantly, tap into your own supply of self-motivation. Movements and organizations are created based on many different areas of interest that all come about and flourish because of the influence of a first-class leader who has passion, conviction, and good organizational skills. The effects can multiply exponentially by spreading the word to many more that who, in turn, can drive achievements even further. Strong or compelling influences that positively affect parents, friends, teachers, siblings, or relatives can all be easily passed on to the younger generation in order to help shape their way of thinking well into the future.

The fact is that young minds are far more easily influenced, and it is this reality that has the world turned upside down in so many areas. Too many negative and destructive influences claim the minds of children, and this has literally changed the shape of humanity as we know it. Young children who start out like everyone else are influenced in various ways into becoming everything from marginal to unthinkable: from selfish and spoiled, to mean and intolerable bullies, all the way down the line to becoming eventual murderers, terrorists, child molesters, and prostitutes. These detrimental influences are fueled in part by fear, fantasy, and greed and render some humans helpless to any resistance.

It is imperative to realize that many sinful humans will gladly sacrifice *your* life for *their* gain without as much as the blink of an eye. What this means is that you and your life are absolutely worthless to them, and your existence bears little or no significance to those whose sole purpose is to achieve an unbreakable influence over the lives of others and exploit them for their own personal gain.

Even worse, a child's soul is often traded for some inhumane cause, fetching nothing more than a few dollars for the perpetrator. Children, such as runaways or those left unsupervised to roam the streets, are often drugged, kidnapped, and then horrifically abused, both mentally and physically, for the sick gratification or emotionless financial gain of immoral criminals.

As an *unattended child*, it can become impossible to fight off all the negative influences around you. They get to you when you are vulnerable and inadequately equipped to defend yourself. Of course, it does not always have to be so dramatic or sinister, but even some subtle influences can leave you a little less prepared to develop your potential.

If you have made it this far, it is of paramount importance to realize that once you are able to make choices or allow yourself to be influenced by others, strangers or not, your fate is in your hands. Be sure to understand the motives of those who influence you in any way.

Your parents, teachers, and friends can protect you only up to a point, and then it is your responsibility to take control and be *smart* about what happens to you next.

Street Smart Tips

- *Don't trust that everyone has your best interest at heart.*
- *Even when people do have good intentions, it is not always possible for them to do the right thing and, consequently, you may become a victim nonetheless.*
- *Everyone is distracted or influenced in one way or another, so it is critical to distinguish the real opportunities from the pitfalls.*

Chapter Twelve

Objectively Speaking

As mentioned once or twice, the most important thing that this book aims to share with you is the significance of being objective about your life. As far-fetched as it may seem, the knack of getting out of your own body and mind and being able to see yourself for who and what you really are is important beyond words.

The ability to use objectivity well leads you to a world where logic and common sense live, where life is simply less complicated and less stressful. Awareness, understanding, and tolerance is the foundation of living a fulfilled life while getting the most out of the cards that you have been dealt. Here, there is no complaining, blaming or whining going on, just a healthy attitude toward doing your best as often as possible.

If you have tried your best throughout the day and are prepared to be just a little productive in any area of your life *each and every day*, then it is safe to say that you should sleep well every night with the knowledge that it will only get better, day after day. Do not allow yourself to waste too many days of your life.

Street Smart Tips

- *A fact is a fact; pretending it's not will not make it go away.*
- *There may not always be a good way but there is usually a best way to fix all problems.*

Who Runs The Show?

Chuck had a nose ring and a visibly colorful tattoo of a bird and a musical note on his neck. This was obviously a very strong statement of independence, and you could not help but stare a little when you first met him. Chuck was, however, no lightweight; he was a nuclear physics graduate from an Ivy League school and passed each class with flying colors.

When Chuck received his PhD, he went on an interview at a major government-operated facility, not too far from where he lived. It was for a supervisory position in the lab, and the pay was more than satisfactory. In fact, if he was fortunate enough to get the job, he would be well-positioned in a very stable career, one that would certainly allow him to pursue some of his more pleasurable goals. He would be able to pay his school loans back in record time and pursue his musical interests. He knew only too well that this was a huge opportunity for him. He was so excited. This was a real break, and life was going to be terrific—he could feel it!

In the lobby Chuck met John, who was also applying for the position. John was a little nerdy to say the least and not exactly Mr. Personality. He had a similar degree but from a local college, not too far from the building that they were in. He was quite nervous for the interview and felt far less confident than Chuck, despite his grades being equally impressive. He was a little unsure if he had what it took to perform as well as the job would require. Other than a quick nod, they made very little eye contact and did not talk to each other at all.

Prof. Carlton, the interviewer, was a tall, thin man sporting a pair of silver-rimmed glasses on the edge of his nose. He wore a gray suit, starched white shirt, and was perfectly groomed with his hair combed neatly to one side. He could hardly hide his surprise when he met Chuck. Even with the very impressive credentials staring up at him from Chuck's résumé; it was quite obvious that Prof. Carlton found it daunting to see beyond the neck tattoo and the nose ring.

But despite being raised in a traditional family and from a small town, Prof. Carlton inexplicably liked Chuck. He could not, however, imagine successfully defending Chuck's appearance to any one of his ultra-conservative colleagues. He was certain that all would frown upon his decision to hire Chuck should he decide to do so, even if he was able to prove beyond a doubt that Chuck was best qualified. Prof. Carlton remained doubtful that Chuck could use his charm or qualifications to win over his colleagues.

Prof. Carlton briefly visualized learning from Chuck about science, physics, and even music; it was apparent that they connected in some small way. Prof. Carlton had a side to him that he mostly kept to himself since he graduated from college and entered the teaching profession. They both had a passion for playing the jazz piano, and both knew how to play many of the same songs. Chuck was unique, and Prof. Carlton felt un-expectantly energized by Chuck.

Needless to say, nerdy John was offered the job. He was a little less qualified, but he looked more like the rest of the staff. Chuck spent the next few months to a year looking for a comparable job, but he never really got over the disappointment from that day. He eventually took a part-time job in a musical instruments store where they seemed a little less concerned with his appearance.

He eventually lost enthusiasm and interest in pursuing his academic field and, although he vowed to get back on track one day, he now has another few tattoos and works a second job at a nightclub downtown. Would he ever know the real cost of his desire to be different or his need to freely express himself? He just happened to be in an environment that was neither ready nor equipped to accept him looking like that.

117

On the one hand, we are really fortunate to live in a country where pretty much anything goes, and diversity is celebrated and accepted by most. On another hand, we are also fortunate to live in a civilized and somewhat organized society which, for the most part, is quite remarkable. How so many diverse people who require such a range of services and specific considerations can live together in relative bliss is beyond comprehension.

Moreover, when compared to most other countries around the world, we take running water, electricity, food, freeways, toilets, garbage disposals, safety, and health services completely for granted. We can even still assume personal safety as a given and so frequently look for the best in people. We are truly fortunate, but is it appreciated enough or will it have to be taken away before the true worth our good fortune is realized?

To achieve and maintain this harmony, there are somewhat ordinary people, just like you and me, who have decided to take on leadership roles and to provide guidance and education not only for themselves, but for their fellow citizens. Because of their desire, education, and qualifications, and most appreciably their willingness to accept great responsibility, these folks exercise the right to influence ordinary citizens and create the rules by which we must all abide. They fight for our rights and often strongly influence the regulations by which we must live. Once you realize what these rules are, what they mean, and how to live within them, you can then focus on taking control of your own destiny and managing your own world within the grand system that has been developed.

We were either born in or have chosen to live in this particular country. Either way, we all live where there are rules. There are in fact fewer limitations in the United States than most other countries in the world, and once you have understood and then mastered these rules and figured out how to play the game of life, you can figure out a way to use the rules to your advantage. To be subjected to reasonable rules and regulations that ensure our safety, peace, and harmony is a noteworthy privilege, a good fortune that many citizens might sometimes mistake for an inconvenience or violation of rights. However, if destabilized, the system under which we live will be unimaginably different because it will all be turned upside down, and nothing short of severe inconvenience and danger will likely follow.

Upside down means taking a *mostly tolerable* environment and turning it into an unprecedented nightmare for everyone. Stop for a moment and think objectively about the many ways in which everything works in your favor, and then, if you will, plan your participation to either improve it or, at a minimum, to keep it that way. If this proves to be too difficult or is unacceptable to you, you may of course choose to live anywhere else in the world and abide by the boundaries and rules of that country and its governing body. I suspect that a place without rules does not exist; at least no place that I believe you would want to live for too long.

So once you really understand who runs the show and can learn to either find a legitimate way to change it or to live under the provided umbrella, taking every educational opportunity into consideration, your life can be prosperous, fulfilling, exciting, and outright enjoyable. By all means, figure out which rules are possible to bend and by how much. Should you want to add a dimension that will prove to be challenging, exciting, and perhaps quite rewarding, go for it!

While we do need structure and order, it is well understood that rules and guidelines, if implemented fairly and used wisely, can be instrumental in the pursuit of your prosperity. If you choose to diversify, that's fine, but proceed with caution. Diversity is encouraged, admired, and welcomed, but the big consideration is whether or not that particular contradiction will cost you more than you can handle. Whether or not you agree or like it, the country is run by seemingly conservative people and those who emulate their beliefs and serve under them.

Some of these people may allow you to mess up your life from time to time because, in reality, they do not care that much about you on any personal level. They provide protection but will not necessarily protect you. It's your life. If you want to fit in the mold, they will let you; if not, you are pretty much on your own and can easily be locked up behind bars, for instance. Freedom comes at a price, always. The system is far from perfect and can always be improved upon, but it is fair to say that it is not as hopeless as it is in many other countries around the globe. Ask yourself whether or not some freedom is better than no freedom at all.

You are certainly encouraged to choose to be free, to embrace diversity, but some thoughtful long-term judgment is often needed to keep the balance. What is cool today may not be so cool tomorrow, so if you are going to do something that will last forever, be sure that you will still want it one day in the distant future, and I mean way down the road. You may try to imagine what I mean by this, and whatever comes to mind is probably true, but, more importantly, I am referring to lost opportunities and most especially the sacrifice of a good education. The need to be different is sometimes just a fad, widely found among young people trying to find their own unique way through life.

You should not condemn people for trying to be different, but, unfortunately, there are those who dislike it a lot and, because they run the show, they are in a position to make one pay dearly for his or her digression from the norm. It is okay to temporarily detour from the "model" so long as the consequences are also provisional, and the reaction is proportionate to the action. Enjoy life, go wild and experiment but always think about abuse, overindulgence, and the long-term effects of your actions, at least once before you pull the trigger.

120

Society changes very slowly in some ways and way too fast in others. Regardless, you are ultimately in charge of what happens to you, your body, and your mind. So, until you are the one running the show, which in this country is still possible, you might reconsider being anti-establishment, particularly when the risks outweigh the rewards.

Again, once you have considered your motives and fully understand the rules and regulations, you can cautiously and intelligently break, manipulate, and twist them. But until you figure out how to do it appropriately, don't be surprised or complain when your freedom is taken away or your privileges are revoked; the people who are actually in charge did not like the way that you behaved.

It often makes sense to postpone today's smaller desires to ensure tomorrow's much greater needs.

Street Smart Tips

- *The safest way to break the rules is to be the one making them.*
- *Ugly is not the 'new attractive'; either make yourself look more appealing or consider not making the change.*
- *The influence of just one person can change your entire destiny, good or bad.*

Logic: Let It Rule!

Kyle knew that he could get hurt riding his bicycle without a helmet because he had been told so many times before. His mom told him as did his dad to never ride without his helmet. It was even right there on the crossbar of his bicycle, a brightly colored sticker from the factory in China warning him of injury or even death should he crash while riding his bicycle without a helmet.

His helmet made his head itch, and the chin strap bothered him and, besides, his friend Jake never wore a helmet and nothing ever happened to him. Kyle hated it so much that he sometimes let it hang over the handlebars when riding short distances. Of course, one day he fell off his bike and hit his head on the curb; he blacked out and when he finally woke up in the emergency room, he started out, words slurring, "I was going to put it on, but I just went around the corner."

His parents just stared at him, tears welling up as they were both unable to speak. Kyle did not yet know that he had damaged a nerve ending on the left side of his brain. The doctors were unsure as to the amount of time it would take to heal; they told his parents that the extent of the damage was hard to gauge and, at this point, a full recovery was not a guarantee. No turning back the clock, no one to blame, if only Kyle had listened to the multiple warnings.

Signs are everywhere. Just look around you and then stop for a minute to think about why someone would go to the trouble, spend the time and expense to make and hang a sign up somewhere. Why do parents, teachers, and law enforcement officers keep warning you about obeying instructions and rules? Why are there such serious punishments for ignoring some signs or laws?

Signs or instructions can be divided into informational, instructional, warning, or mandatory advice. What they have in common is that they are typically for the benefit or safety of all humans. They help us to better manage our own lives and protect the lives of others. The more that people ignore signs, the sooner they move from one category to another. A sign that is initially informative may become mandatory because we live in a world where logic often escapes us, sometimes leading to severe consequences for others. It is not uncommon for people to get hurt or killed an important piece of advice was ignored, and it usually happens right at the location where the sign can be found swaying in the wind.

Equally important are the many virtual signs that can be interpreted to make your life much better. These signs can be in the form of body language, gestures, indirect comments, and suggestions, and if understood correctly and acted upon appropriately, they can do much to improve relationships, help you seize opportunities, and enhance your overall well-being. This is a vital component of the street-smart advantage under discussion.

Logic is often described as sound and reasonable judgment, but it is sometimes difficult for people to let logic govern their choices because of the external factors, such as excitement, emotion, rage, or frustration, which interfere. If we were able to exercise logic at all times, the world as we know it would be a very different place.

Now bear in mind, there is the world that we all live in, and then, there is *your* world.

It is usually a good idea to allow as much logic into your world as possible. Often what works well in your world can benefit everyone around you. If you play it reasonably safe, no one gets hurt. If you are reckless and self-centered, innocent people around you might be worse off for knowing you. When in doubt about solving any important dilemma, first consider allowing a little logic to guide you.

A shot or two of simple reasoning will more often than not come to your aid when you attempt any daunting task. Ask yourself the following effective question before taking the leap: *"What are the possible outcomes if I do it this way or if I choose to do it that way?"* ☺ (This is the question mentioned in the Foreword) and then, based on your level of comfort with the most probable outcome, make your decision and stick to it. Don't allow yourself to be influenced by others or by a temporary bout of emotion.

Try to make all tough decisions with a level head or, if necessary, put it off for a little while until you are calmer and have had time to reflect. Of course, in a perfect world, having more knowledge is always an advantage when facing critical choices, but having adequate information is not always possible. It is undoubtedly best to find out as much as you can about any given situation before making final commitments to act. This can be said about almost anything. Failing that option, you will have to count on your gut feelings, possible experience, common sense, and a little faith.

Research is an important prerequisite to all sound decision making, specifically when it comes to making career choices, deciding where to live, who to marry, or anything that will apply to a significant part of your life. Find out all you can even if you think that you already know because things do change, and you may not have received the memo. The worst case is that you confirm that what you know is still valid. As a bonus, you might discover new and useful information.

Uncovering facts you did not know that you did not know could save you all kinds of trouble, especially if it is information that you wish weren't true. You are bound to find out bad news sooner or later, so why wait until you have already invested substantial time, money, and sweat, only to start all over again? This is bonus learning, and it is this type of education that keeps one moving forward in the right direction. One of the challenges that parents face when coaching, teaching, or guiding their young children is that kids sometimes do not know what they do not know, and so they become defensive and agitated. They believe that they already know everything, and so they won't listen to sound advice. It becomes extremely difficult to connect or to have a constructive discussion, leaving the 'teacher' extremely frustrated and then eventually giving up, often when it is about something that is potentially life threatening to you.

It is considered *smart* to approach any subject or task by first asking yourself what more there is to learn about the project before jumping in with both feet. Likewise, if a young person is lucky enough to find a mentor or a role model who has his or her best interests at heart, it is best to first listen a lot, make arguments, ask more questions, and then make decisions with a much greater sensibility. It can sometimes be overwhelming for parent and child or student and teacher because there is much to know about everything, and even the most educated and well-respected men and women don't always have all the answers to everything.

It is a great idea to write down and then look up every new word you hear throughout the day, whether it's overheard or written somewhere. Any opportunity to find out a little something new about anything every day is truly an accumulation of wealth. Even seemingly random or boring data on some level might help you sometime in the future. From impressing someone influential, to gaining an advantage, to winning a contract, to preserving a life— perhaps even your own—education will never hurt you.

You can typically never learn too much and seldom ever regret having had an education. As mentioned before in this book, book smarts together with street smarts will ensure that you have a much richer journey. This in itself is logical; the more you know and the better you are prepared to use your knowledge at the right time and at the right place, the more chance you will have at enjoying an awesome life. Education alone will not guarantee a hassle-free experience, but what you know and have discovered along the way, sprinkled with a good dose of common sense, can make you one of the "lucky" few who gets to enjoy some of life's finer pleasures. By now you know that I do not just mean a flashy car or a dazzling yacht, but rather some of the amazing things that money cannot buy. For those who need a reminder, I am referring to such gifts as peace of mind, love, respect, friendship, security, and some time off to really appreciate what nature has to offer.

On the most basic level, education and a reasonable outlook can help you avoid some of the mistakes, pitfalls, and destructive hurdles that have taken the life out of the living for so many unfortunate people in this world. If you currently have the choice to be free and the opportunity to learn, it is simply not rational to jeopardize it in any way.

Remember, a sign that says DANGER usually came about after someone died or was badly injured. A sign that offers directions was created after someone got lost. Overall, education is humankind's way of saying, "We tried every which way until we got it right; and this is how you do it."

People sometimes wonder why, if they keep on doing the same things over and over again, they get the same results. Take notes, read the signs, follow directions, and heed warnings. Take advantage of your ability to use good judgment, and then share your knowledge and good fortune with others, as others have done with you; this is how we keep our worlds on the right track. Being surrounded by other well-informed and satisfied people is not all bad, considering some of the alternatives that we have come to know too well.

Be *smart* and pay careful attention to all signs, both physical and virtual, for what might happen to you when you ignore them is the very reason that they exist in the first place!

Street Smart Tips

- *People typically like to say, "I told you so!" Don't let them.*
- *It is stupid to blame anyone else for your own stupidity.*
- *A warning is not against you; it is actually for you.*

Chapter Thirteen

How Long Do You Want To Live?

Mrs. Jones is an 89-year-old widow who fell ill one day to a common ailment that was easily recognizable and curable, and so she went to see her doctor. While she was being examined, the doctor found that she had a few other routine problems but assured her that with new medical breakthroughs, she would be fine and that he could prescribe some medication that, when taken twice a day, would keep her going for many years to come. This was of course great news, other than the fact that this new medicine was expensive and not covered by her insurance.

Mrs. Jones, like so many other elderly folks, had limited resources but had not spent much time during her life thinking about this particular predicament. She certainly could not easily decide whether or not she should spend the little money that she had left in her savings on this new medicine to keep her alive for a while longer. What was she to do?

She figured that her limited monthly income would cover only the cost of half the required dose of her prescription, and so she would either not really get better fast enough, or she could just not take it and risk becoming really sick, or worse, dying sooner—just to have enough money for her basic needs, like food and rent.

Her one and only son, with whom she rarely communicated, lived in a small, one-bedroom apartment in another state, but he too was financially unsound, making it impossible to help her in any meaningful way. Even if she were able to go and live with him to avoid living on the streets, the thought of leaving everything behind, giving up her one and only good friend and her beloved dog, to live in very difficult conditions in a strange town was simply unbearable.

Mrs. Jones was financially and emotionally unprepared to live for much longer under these conditions, despite the medical technology available to keep her alive for years to come. What a sad state of affairs to have to deal with at such a tender age.

These predicaments are not uncommon and affect more and more senior citizens in greater numbers every year. If you are not healthy, happy, or in control of your life and finances, you may be one who will simply outlive your income, desires, and usefulness. What misery to look forward to—seriously.

At the end of it all, no one really wants to become a burden to others, but it is becoming unavoidable and inevitable for so many in these times, and the odds are not in favor of improving any time soon. It is more important than ever to plan ahead and to do it as early as possible so that you can secure the ability to maintain basic human needs when you get old.

These are basics such as a roof over your head, food to eat, hot water to bathe in, clothes to wear, necessary medicines to ease pain or to avoid catastrophic ailments, and then with a giant spoon of luck, you can still enjoy emotional ties with family and friends and some travel to faraway places. Even if it is probable that you will be fine in the future, there are no guarantees because people squander fortunes all the time, destroy healthy relationships, and, therefore, assuming the status quo forever can prove to be somewhat foolish.

You are not encouraged to expect the worst, but it would not be a bad idea to plan for it, just in case. The best case scenario is that you have too much money and you don't really need it all when you are older. This is not a bad situation in which to find yourself, I might add. The opposite is of course unthinkable. Just imagine not having enough money to live on and being too old, too sick, or too tired to work, even if some meaningless job was to be had.

Living well and enjoying a long life will ultimately depend on your physical and mental health, but let's not forget the importance of your financial well-being and the ability to support your lifestyle when the time comes. Consider that the length and quality of your life may depend greatly on how you have lived your life and the *smart* choices that you have made along the way.

Street Smart Tips

- *Compound interest is one of the world's marvels; do the math, and start saving young—start now!*
- *If you spend all that you earn and live beyond your means when you are young, you will most likely struggle when you are older.*
- *If you have too much, give some away; the rewards are immeasurable.*

Creating Your Life Story

Some people would do anything they could for you, but it will likely never be enough. So, it is critical that you remain accountable for what happens to you in life. You can't reasonably expect to just wake up one day and be all set until the day you die. Even winning the lottery will not do that for you. Once you understand and accept the actual implication of *reality*, you can prepare for the creation and the protection of your own life story.

Whatever happens next is going to take place in *your world*, which just happens to be an unimaginably small part of our planet.

Your current reality is only somewhat predetermined by what you have to start out with, but it is what you are going to do with all your resources that really matters—so that you, too, can realize your dreams, no matter what. Every major decision that you make from now on will go toward the making of your own unique life story. Little decisions will hardly make any difference, but many of the more profound choices will make a powerful and everlasting mark on your journey.

When you look back one day, and you will, what will you see, and will you like it? What do you want to become, and what will need to be accomplished so that you can be successful in achieving that goal?

There are still many good options to choose from in life, and by choosing a few of them along the way, you will undoubtedly make significant improvements to your life. Sure, street smarts have typically been learned by knocking your head or bruising your ego, but there are more than a few ways in which one can learn these skills. Formal education is typically essential to operate at the highest levels, but it can be very demanding and not guarantee anything. The best formal education today is by-and-large not affordable to everyone, and so this avenue can be frustrating. While others seem to have everything going their way, it is not *just* their expensive Ivy League education at play.

As vital as a formal education is, more important is the acquisition of *social dexterity*, a critical but learnable science that uses logic and common sense infused with self-respect and a healthy dose of self-motivation. This is the formula for self-confidence, the key to progress.

How do you go about learning street smarts? The first step is easy; simply start watching what other people are doing, noticing how they behave and, in particular, how it makes you feel, especially those who seem to have it all together, even if it is just at first glance. For the easiest lessons, you would typically be on the lookout for someone who obviously (the not-so-obvious is level two of street smarts) enjoys a somewhat pleasant family life; one who is well-groomed, well-spoken, and well-established with reliable transportation; and one who lives in a pretty safe neighborhood, all while demonstrating plenty of self-confidence and generosity. This person is probably quite content evidenced by a caring nature and friendliness toward others.

Last, but by no means least, they will come across as fairly well-educated, which is intentionally mentioned last so that you will remember it well. It is very important to realize that education *in any form* is a priority and will take you the farthest in achieving the many goals that are currently swirling around in your head.

It is a huge mistake to underestimate the power of useful knowledge. There is an overwhelming amount of knowledge everywhere, now more than ever before in unimaginable proportion. Whatever you need to know can be found instantaneously and, once it is sorted carefully, it can be used to prepare you for virtually every situation possible. With the right knowledge and enough self-motivation, you can master your own destiny. But be aware that there is information to seek out and information to avoid. Your task will be to differentiate between the two and to put the knowledge that you need for your own achievements to good use.

To keep it interesting, everything that you do learn could potentially lead you to undiscovered areas of fascination (we do not know what we do not know!), and that is what makes proactive living exciting. By continuously striving to learn more every day, regardless of the platform or the topic, you may inadvertently be led down an avenue that allows you to discover and realize your full potential.

Newfound inspiration may afford you the opportunity of living in this world with adoration and respect from another human. This quest to learn as much as you possibly can might allow you to discover a previously unknown break that may well turn an ordinary life into an extraordinary one. *Your happiness may depend solely on your attitude toward learning.*

So without being too weird, let's stop and think for a minute about your eulogy one fine day in the very distant future. For those who are unfamiliar with the term or the concept—and you ought to be for as long as possible—this is the final sermon created for you and about you when you finally leave this world.

What will people say about you after you die? This speech is usually delivered by a person or people who know you best and have had the pleasure of your friendship or the distinct honor of being related to you for as far back as they can remember. What they say about you will be their summation of your entire life, whether it is factual or perceived. All they can say about you will be wrapped up in twenty minutes or less. Given the choice, which you still have, what would you like that final speech to say about you, considering it is how people will remember you? It will be specifically about what your entire existence meant to everyone who was associated with you in one way or another.

Let's assume that you will be fortunate enough to have more than a few loved ones stand up in front of everybody at your funeral and say something about you. Given what you know right now, what will you honestly expect them to say?

Street Smart Tips

- *When putting things off until later, we are simply adding to what will need to be done then.*
- *Successful people do the things that unsuccessful people are not prepared to do.*
- *When you eventually get what you want, you will most likely want something else, so make sure that the sacrifices you made were well worth it.*
- *Your money will never buy you happiness but it can buy some for someone else.*

Is Getting Old Looking Good?

One of the most fascinating ways to manage your life is to try and paint a picture of what you will be doing when you reach a ripe old age. I realize that this is one of the hardest things for young people to do because they believe that they have plenty of time, things will change, and that because they are too young to know what they want to do, it can wait. This is, unfortunately, a very costly way to think.

Most older people look back and admit that they wish they had started saving earlier, studied more, taken more chances, listened to more advice, and generally not waited so long to take care of important things. They all would have acted a little sooner had they believed then that they would simply run out of time or energy necessary to achieve many of their goals.

Take a moment and think about it. Do you one day want to be the coolest grandparent on the planet, a humble philanthropist, a frustrated parking lot attendant, a famous entertainer, a motivational educator, or the resident manager of one of the government-housing projects in your state, the one in which you reside? How about being an awesome [insert whatever you want to be], enjoying the ride and then leaving a mark of distinction on this world, something so *wow* that you will be fondly remembered every time your name comes up in conversation?

Maybe you'll enjoy the ambience of a large family with many grandchildren running around; financial security for you, your spouse, and your kids; the satisfaction of self-respect; the tranquility of honor; the joy of good friends; the opportunity to travel to exotic places; or simply having the accessibility to loved ones. So, ask yourself what the necessary steps might be and what actions, if coordinated today, will most likely lead you to the realization of these enviable goals.

Just like anything else in life, there are instructions, recipes, guidelines, and recommended paths and, most importantly, many good ideas that came from people who lived before you. Together with the belief in yourself, hard work, tenacity, honesty, dignity, reliability, and a little help from your friends, you can begin a journey today that may well turn out to be the very way you plan it.

What makes life interesting and adventurous is all the twists and turns along the way, and if you give it your best shot and mostly do the right things, mostly avoid many of the pitfalls, and most of all never give up, you *might* just live to see all of your dreams come true. It is, however, safe to say that if you don't do any of the above, you most likely won't.

Everybody needs a lift in life; your task is to simply be the type of person that someone would want to help.

Street Smart Tips

- *Failing to plan is planning to fail.*
- *If you buy a lottery ticket, you have something like a 0.000000001 percent chance of winning, but if you don't, you have a 100 percent chance that you won't.*
- *If you believe that you can, you are right; and if you believe that you can't, you are also right.*

Chapter Fourteen

If Only I Knew Then...

Kimberly went out on more than one occasion alone and late at night. Over the years, she had overheard a few horror stories of young girls getting roughed up or raped by seemingly innocent-looking boys, but she did not believe that her town was home to any of these dangerous creatures and just brushed this off as she casually went about her business.

Despite the deep-seated concerns of her older sister and her parents, they never really brought up the subject more than once or twice, and Kimberly continued gallivanting and making lots of new friends at the local bar with her carefree, flirtatious demeanor. These were of course mostly boys, but they seemed innocent enough and did not make her feel uncomfortable in any way.

Kimberly, although just seventeen years old, easily passed for a little older and was typically never questioned when ordering a drink or two at the bar. One particular evening, she met an unfamiliar boy who explained how he had recently moved into town because of his father's new promotion. He and his family had to transfer to her town, but he told her that it was a new and exciting opportunity for his dad, and he was keen to learn all about the new town that he would now be calling home.

Kimberly took a liking to Mark and offered to show him around the next day. He seemed pleasant and respectful and wasn't bad looking either. Pretty soon, and in a gentlemanly fashion, he offered to walk her home. She gladly accepted and therefore stayed at the bar a little later than usual. Her parents were at home a little concerned that she was still out so late, until she called to assure them she was fine and she was being escorted home. Not able to stay awake any longer, they both went to sleep and were soon snoring.

Not long after the police found Kimberly's body, just as the sun was rising, it was quickly discovered that Mark was in town on the run from the police in a neighboring state. He had a previous record for the sexual assault of at least four other young girls. It turns out that on the way back to Kimberly's home, he became agitated when she declined his advances to go into the park and, while struggling to free herself from his grip, she lost her balance falling backward and randomly hitting her head on a sharp rock. Mark fled the scene in a panic. Kimberly would never be able to tell anyone what really happened that night.

Mark was picked up near the border and within hours was in custody and behind bars, but it was too late for Kimberly. One way or the other, she was in for a very terrifying night. She was unsuspecting and therefore not careful enough; she could have taken the warnings by her family a little more seriously, but she never did want to hear them. Had she given a little extra thought to the situation and come to realize that it could potentially turn out to be dangerous, she may still be alive.

If only she were just a little older, a little more sensible or aware, if only she weren't so naive or stubborn. But now, it's simply too late for tears...if only.

Sometimes we are very fortunate and get to brush off misfortune or danger with nothing but a little scare, but on other occasions it turns out to be heartbreaking. We can't know what might have been had we not ignored important information. There are no guarantees, and some people just don't escape.

But we all have an automatic mechanism to help us to not focus on negative or stressful concepts for too long. Any continuous significant problem that hangs over us has to eventually be put aside at some point; otherwise, it will get too heavy and blow our minds. Humans can learn how to ignore many of the potentially relentless drains on our lives. Some use natural methods to help them forget, and there are those who use artificial stimulants.

Either way, the problem won't just go away; but those who maintain a clearer mind and show the most determination will most likely achieve the necessary steps to remove the problem. Be aware that many seemingly insignificant problems may get bigger and bigger the longer you wait; they seldom, if ever, just disappear.

Consider not putting off anything important. The worse the chore or the harder the challenge, the quicker it should be eliminated for good. This will save a lot of stress and anxiety in the future.

Let' face it. Many people would love to have a second chance to live their lives knowing what they now know. Like a few other facts we must accept in life, it is outright impossible to turn back the clock, but there is a very good alternative, well worth a good look.

Every young person growing up and embracing the world has **two profound challenges to overcome**, which is a huge part of what makes life interesting, stimulating, and exhilarating but, embracing them is <u>WHAT WILL MAKE THE DIFFERENCE!</u>

If you learn to first understand and then master these two challenges, you can create a much better life for yourself, better than the one that you are currently on track to accept.

<u>The first major challenge</u> is that young (and not so young) people simply believe they *cannot or need not* look into the future and visualize themselves as older and established. Kids typically don't really *want* to take the time until they have to. So, they choose to either ignore the blurry little pictures in their heads or to postpone watching them for as long as possible. It is after all much easier to gamble on your future than to make the necessary sacrifices and to do some of what it takes when you are still young.

You may think that because youth is on your side that there is plenty of time to get around to it, and that living one day in the future *will* be in accordance with your plan because you are programmed to believe that things will take care of themselves.

Overwhelmingly more often than not, plans change drastically along the way. The probability that you will travel down roads and around corners that you now have no idea even exist is very real. The best course of action is to be as prepared as possible for whatever comes your way. Imagine it and it can happen to you, even if it only happens years from now.

By all means, believe in yourself and your ability to take care of yourself and your family one day, but you can be better prepared, always. Ask any adult; time flies, new adventures or obligations distract you, people you haven't yet met will strongly persuade you, and so some pre-planned, must-have opportunities in your life will simply be missed.

Procrastination will guarantee a little regret with each passing day. At the very least, consider some of what it might take to secure your future—today.

The second major challenge to overcome is that you will miss major opportunities because you *did not have* the required knowledge or information at the time that you needed it most. Granted, you did not know that it existed until you needed it, but the information or solution was always available; it is just that you chose not to take the necessary steps to discover it in advance.

If you know about something before you are forced to learn about it, the results are usually very different and typically in your favor. Be open-minded to everything, even if it seems unnecessary to learn it at that particular time. READ as much as possible about everything you can at *every* opportunity.

An adventurous spirit can be extra exciting for some daredevil types, but in the context of living in modern times, it is usually better knowing something before rather than after the fact under most circumstances. Many a financial catastrophe, heartbreak, or worse might have been avoided with prior experience, knowledge, or a fair warning. Perhaps the information was there for you to grasp but you missed it, ignored it, or chose to take the easy way out.

Some kids today are considered extremely smart, specifically because they have decided to *make a special effort* and to listen better, watch more, read more and take more notes. They try to understand most everything that they witness and experience. This is intellect at work—clever strategizing and smart planning.

They choose to emulate the actions of others; those they believe will make their lives safer, more worthwhile and fulfilling in the future. They seek knowledge, study, save, exercise, have self-respect, build trust, maintain solid relationships, appreciate, and also understand how it all works; they just plain get it. They understand that there are learning opportunities everywhere in every corner of their existence.

Everywhere they are, everywhere they have been, and everywhere they are going, they find something worthwhile to ponder, if only for a moment. They pay attention, are alert and think clearly. They are open-minded and can process information and extract the lesson instantly. Moreover, they understand balance and the detriments of focusing on the wrong things at the wrong time.

They learn from good people as well as from dreadful and indifferent people; they take what they need to create a logical, peaceful, safe, and content world for themselves. These kids are *street smart*, humble, and grateful. They share, they teach, and they take in all that life has to offer them. They simply get their fill!

The perpetual questioning and processing of all experiences, information, and assumptions is what you might call learning *street smarts* (or *wisdom* when you are older).

Again, college, university, or any higher education is preferred—no ifs, ands, or buts. However, there is also a vital education available to you every day, wherever you go. The most common way to gain street smarts is well-known and referred to as "hard knocks" or personal mistakes, but this takes time and resources that we often can't afford, and it can wreak havoc on an unprepared person of any age.

A widely available resource-filled alternative to consider is learning from the *experiences or mistakes of others*. There are many adults who have already made more than half of your mistakes for you. They will gladly share their experiences with you, if you just let them. Just ask or seek out the information from older people. They would love to help anyone who will listen to them; they will share their stories that are full of useful lessons. It is a win-win all the way. So many older people have a lot to share but, like life itself, it's not all going to be high-energy stimulation all the time. But hang in there because you are destined to find a little gold in every encounter.

By simply raising your level of situational awareness—that is, by attentively watching what works and what doesn't for others and then questioning it—you can make noticeable improvements in many aspects of your life. Friendly warning devices exist all around us; we call them grown-ups. You'll also find helpful information around every corner, and it just makes good sense to hear it, read it, and remember it.

Hopefully, many of your mentors will behave in ways that prove good choices have better results. When we stop ignoring important information, we all take a giant leap forward in improving our lives. Learning by hard knocks is overrated. You cannot avoid them altogether, but many of these hard knocks leave a long-lasting, negative effect that can take years to forget.

Again, formal education is advisable, but without learning street smarts, taking on the world will likely be a far more frustrating venture. But it does not have to be. Neither form of education comes without expense, dedication, and effort, but both are certainly a lot less painful and less costly than the alternatives. Taking the easy way out today almost always guarantees the hard way tomorrow.

Be aware of everything around you and take full advantage because every single day someone else is out there making mistakes so that you don't have to. Just watch them and learn!

Street Smart Tips

- *Your grandparents or your friend's grandparents have good information that you really want to know; just ask them.*
- *Working hard is admirable; working smart is enviable.*
- *Remember to learn something, every day. It will be a surprising advantage one day when you least expect it.*

First Love Yourself, and then Pass It On!

Start a deeper conversation about any of the following topics by going to:

www.streetsmartkids.com

1. The future isn't what it used to be.
2. We are born perfect, but it's downhill from there.
3. Parents' responsibilities and shortcomings.
4. Your responsibilities and shortcomings.
5. Objectivity: Who really runs the show?
6. Balance: the art of pacing yourself.
7. Your body, as a machine, needs the right fuel.
8. Find your comfort zone.
9. Bad habits, the worst one of all.
10. If only I knew then what I know now.
11. If you can, you must!
12. Learning both bad and good things.
13. Exposed to adult content while still immature.
14. Being a kid for as long as possible.
15. Being a parent and changing diapers.
16. The quality of friends and peers.
17. Peer pressure—is good.
18. Taking the easy way out.
19. Impressing your friends with stupidity.
20. Sincerity will take you far in life.
21. The end—what would you say about you?
22. Lucky to be healthy.
23. Being clever versus smart versus intelligent.
24. Born athletic, the pros and cons?

25. Caring for our bodies (hardware).
26. Caring for our minds (software).
27. How long will you live?
28. Risks—which ones are worthwhile?
29. Future leaders—are you just going to watch?
30. Personal hygiene.
31. Reliability creates opportunity.
32. Accountability is not the same as responsibility.
33. Early Independence.
34. Relationships—better life for each other first.
35. Body language—reaction.
36. Do unto others.
37. Successful people do the things that...
38. Ignoring important information.
39. Signs are everywhere.
40. Putting others down.
41. Bullying shows that you have serious problems.
42. Stress is dangerous.
43. Giving without expectations.
44. Others are worse off than you.
45. Where you live in the world, your community.
46. Luck: where preparation meets opportunity.
47. Creating versus wishing.
48. Taking things for granted.
49. Medicine can kill you.
50. Divorce—living through it.
51. Immigrant parents and what is good about it.
52. Procrastination—the price.
53. We are all three people. Strive to be just one.
54. First impressions last far too long.

55. Manners: the cost of not having any.

56. Racism—living through it.

57. Respecting elders: the benefits are huge.

58. Putting things back where you find them.

59. Borrowing—the hidden opportunity it presents.

60. Russian Roulette: play it and lose big.

61. Risk versus Reward.

62. Consequences—always.

63. Admitting your mistakes—big benefits.

64. Sleeping well at night.

65. Honesty and integrity.

66. Are you a flake?

67. Punctuality—what's so important about it?

68. Tattoos.

69. Public bathrooms.

70. Washing your hands.

71. Brushing your teeth.

72. Humor at others' expense.

73. Spitting in public.

74. Win-Win.

75. If you think you can...

76. Too much of a good thing.

77. Graffiti in public places.

78. Managing yourself vs. being managed by others.

79. People are treated as objects.

80. Assumptions from credentials: life is not fair.

81. Do what you say you are going to do, always.

82. Safety in the kitchen and bathroom.

83. Good looks.

84. Trust; important beyond words.

85. Lucky breaks.

86. Tolerance.

87. Why is patience so important?

88. Complaining.

89. Parents do try.

90. Do the best you can, always.

91. Creating your own unique life story.

92. Hating work and chores.

93. One step at a time.

94. Wanting what others have.

95. The strong prey on the weak.

96. If you think education is expensive, try ignorance.

97. The importance of 'self-everything'.

98. Gifts that remain unopened.

99. Do you get it?